knitstyle

chic and sexy accessories

Barbara W. Larson

CRE▲TIVE
HOMEOWNER® Home Arts

We are gareful to Lion Brand Yarn Co. who granted permission to reprint the following patterns: Classic Beret – "kim-beret" (unnumbered), Faux Fur Capelet/Chenille Collar – "Knitted Capelet" (Pattern Number: 40431), and Ruffled Scarf – "Spiral 'Ruffled' Scarf" (Pattern Number: 50193-1C).

Thick and Quick® and Wool-Ease® are registered trademarks of Lion Brand Yarn.

KNIT STYLE: CHIC AND SEXY ACCESSORIES

SENIOR EDITOR: Carol Endler Sterbenz
SENIOR DESIGNER: Glee Barre
ASSISTANT EDITOR: Evan Lambert
PHOTO RESEARCHER: Robyn Poplasky
TECHNICAL EDITORS: Karin Strom, Eve Ng, Cheryl Krementz
ASSISTANT DESIGNER: Stephanie Phelan
DIAGRAMS: Diane P. Smith-Gale
COVER DESIGN: Glee Barre
INDEXER: Schroeder Indexing Services
FASHION PHOTOGRAPHY: Damian Sandone
INSTRUCTIONAL PHOTOGRAPHY: Marta and Ben Curry
CONTRIBUTING PHOTOGRAPHER: Steven Mays

CREATIVE HOMEOWNER

VP/PUBLISHER: Brian Toolan
VP/EDITORIAL DIRECTOR: Timothy O. Bakke
PRODUCTION MANAGER: Kimberly H. Vivas
ART DIRECTOR: David Geer
MANAGING EDITOR: Fran J. Donegan

Printed in China

Current Printing (last digit)
10 9 8 7 6 5 4 3 2 1

Knit Style: Chic and Sexy Accessories, First Edition
Library of Congress Control Number: 2006922057
ISBN-10: 1-58011-305-2
ISBN-13: 978-1-58011-305-2

CREATIVE HOMEOWNER®
A Division of Federal Marketing Corp.
24 Park Way
Upper Saddle River, NJ 07458
www.creativehomeowner.com

dedication

To my precious family,
with special thanks to my
husband, Andy, whose willing and
unflagging support confirms that love
is indeed a verb.

table of contents

introduction

Knitting is one of life's great pleasures, providing a ready vehicle for artistic expression. With knitting, we get to combine colors and textures to create a thing of beauty.

In **KNIT STYLE** you will be given a choice of more than 25 great-looking items, each one knitted in today's most popular yarns and gathered in "The Collection." This section features fashion faves such as a flirty scarf with a profusion of pom-poms, a shrug with faux fur collar and cuffs, a chunky ponchette, a cool purse, and much, much more. Each knitted item is accompanied by a stylistic variation, giving you an even greater

the collection

choice of looks in items that are sure to become wardrobe staples.

KNIT STYLE includes the indispensable "Knitting Basics" and "Sources & Resources," two sections that provide all the essential information you will need to ensure great knitting experiences. Notable is **KNIT STYLE**'s format, an easel-back, spiral bound book for "hands-free" knitting.

You will find in **KNIT STYLE** that there is something inexpressibly gratifying about using your hands to knit fiber into fabric that is both lovely and useful; it's not exactly weaving straw into gold, but it's close.

Barbara W. Larson

7

pink gardenia pin

a versatile accessory!

Creating a flower accessory—what fun! Even though particular yarns and beads are listed here, this should by no means cramp your style. Use your scrap yarn and bead collections for a one-of-a-kind creation. There is no right way to make a flower; in fact, no two will look alike, but that's a good thing!

SKILL LEVEL
Basic

MEASUREMENTS
Approx. 4½" (11cm) in diameter

MATERIALS
- 61 yds. (55.8m) medium-weight rayon microfiber/wool blend (one ball Muench Yarns "Touch Me" in #3642 pink) (A)
- 153 yds. (140m) fine-weight nylon (one ball Katia "Sevilla" in #54 canteloupe) (B)
- 82 yds. (75m) bulky-weight nylon (one ball Gedifra "Cubetto" in #1106 red mix) (C)
- Pair of US 10 (6mm) needles
- Tapestry needle
- Sewing needle and matching thread
- One 1½" (3.8cm) button
- One pin back
- Optional: beads, beading needle and thread.

GAUGE
3 sts to 1" (2.5cm) measured over st st on US 10 (6mm) needles (or size to obtain gauge).

ABBREVIATIONS
See page 82.

PIN

Petals (make 3)

With A, cast on 3 sts. leaving a 5-in. (12.7cm) tail.

Row 1 (WS): K.

Row 2: P.

Row 3 (inc): Kfb, k1, kfb. [5 sts]

Row 4 (inc): Pfb, p to the last st, pfb. [7 sts]

Row 5 (inc): Kfb, k to the last st, kfb. [9 sts]

Row 6 and all RS rows: P.

Rows 7, 9, 11, 13, 15, 17, 19 and 21 (inc): K1, kfb, k to last 2 sts, kfb, k1. [25 sts after row 21]

Row 23: K.

Row 24 (dec): P1, p2tog, p to the last 3 sts, p2tog, p1. [23 sts]

Row 25 (dec): K1, k2tog, k to the last 3 sts, k2tog, k1. [21 sts]

Rows 26-33: Repeat rows 24-25. [5 sts after row 33.]

Row 34: P1, p2tog, p2. [4 sts]

Row 35: K1, k2tog, k1. [3 sts]

BO, leaving a 5-in. (12.7cm) tail.

FINISHING

1. Thread the tail into tapestry needle, and using a running st, sew up the center of petal toward the cast-on edge.
2. Pull on the tail so the petal ruches, and knot it to secure it.
3. Arrange the petals with the tail ends tog, and secure them using B.
4. Shape the petals as desired, using a sewing needle and thread to tack them in place on the WS.
5. Make a 2-in. (5.1cm) tassel using B and C, and attach it to the center of the flower.
6. Sew the button to the center of flower, over tassel, and/or embellish it as desired.
7. Sew a pin back onto the back of flower, adding a dab of glue to secure it.

Petal Diagram

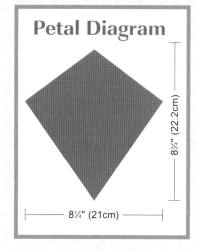

8¾" (22.2cm)

8¼" (21cm)

TIP

Use smaller needles and lighter-weight yarn for a more delicate version.

Style Variation

Floral embellishments are seen everywhere—on hats, bags, scarves, and belts. For a designer look, fasten color-coordinated miniature blooms to your shoes. Remember—it's all in the details.

lacy
choker

with ribbon

streamers

T he lacy choker is worked in a moss stitch that lends textural interest to the section encircling the neck. The long ribbon streamers in variegated gem colors can be worn as a bow at the side of the neck or allowed to fall gracefully over the bodice. Wherever they are, these hand-dyed ribbons will be gorgeous.

SKILL LEVEL
Basic

MEASUREMENTS
- Length: 12" (30cm), excluding beads and ties
- Width: 3½" (9cm)

MATERIALS
- 83 yds. (76m) bulky-weight nylon/microfiber blend {one skein Artfibers "Biscotti" [1.8 oz. (50g)], #15 burnt orange} (A)
- 127 yds. (116m) medium-weight cotton {one ball Artfibers "Papyrus" [1¾ oz. (50g)], #14 purple} (B)
- 100 yds. (91m) superbulky-weight nylon {one ball Artfibers "Houdini" [3 oz. (86g)], #4 multi-color} (C)
- Pair US 9 (5.5mm) needles
- Two 3-hole bar beads, 27x6mm
- Six 8mm round beads
- Crochet hook
- Needle threader

GAUGE
14 sts and 22 rows to 4" (10cm) measured over moss stitch on US 9 (5.5mm) needles.

ABBREVIATIONS
See page 82.

LACY CHOKER

Using A, cast on 11 sts.
Rows 1 and 4: K1, *p1, k1; rep from * to the end.
Rows 2 and 3: *P1, k1; rep from * to the last st, p1.
Rows 4-64: Rep rows 1-4.
Row 65: Rep row 1.
BO foll row 2 of the pattern.

TOP AND BOTTOM BORDERS

Decide which side will be your RS, and mark it with a safety pin.
With B and RS facing, pick up 42 sts across one long edge.
Row 1: K.
Row 2: P.
BO k-wise. Rep on the opposite edge.

SIDE BORDERS

With B and RS facing, pick up 12 sts across one side edge, including the top and bottom borders.
Row 1: K.
Row 2: P.
BO k-wise. Rep on the opposite edge.

RIBBON TIES

Cut six 60-in. (152cm) strands of C. Attach three fringes to each short end. Thread the fringes through the bar bead. Make a knot close to the bead to secure it; then thread a fringe through each round bead, and secure them with knots.

Style Variation

The featured choker is long enough to be worn as a belt. Its saturated jewel colors make it the perfect counterpoint to a peasant skirt in rich purple velvet. Allow the belt to fall slightly below your waist, and tie the streamers in a soft bow.

classic
beret

stylish

no matter

the season

A classic beret takes on a contemporary flair when it is worn in a jaunty way. Knit in the round, the soft-to-the-touch cashmere blend makes the beret comfortable to wear. Pair it with a dressy leather jacket or with a comfortable turtleneck sweater and trousers. Or knit it in a color that matches a dressy coat.

SKILL LEVEL
Intermediate

MEASUREMENTS
Diameter: 10" (25.4cm), after blocking
Fits average adult head: 21-23" (53.3-58.4cm)

MATERIALS
- 168 yds. (154m) medium-weight cashmere or cashmere blend {two balls Lion Brand "Lion Cashmere Blend" [1¼ oz. (40g)], #124 camel}
- One US 6 (4.25mm) 16" (40.6cm) circular needle
- Set of five US 6 (4.25mm) double-pointed needles (dpns)
- Six stitch markers
- Tapestry needle

GAUGE
18 sts and 30 rows to 4" (10cm) measured over st st on US 6 (4.25mm) needles (or size to obtain gauge).

ABBREVIATIONS
See page 82.

BERET

BRIM

With circular needle and A, cast on 76 sts. Mark beg of rnd with stitch marker, and join, being careful not to twist the sts.

Rnd 1: *K1, p1; rep from * to end of rnd.

Rep rnd 1 for 1½ in. (3.8cm).

Inc rnd: *K1, kfb; rep from * to end of rnd. [114 sts]

Work in St st (k every rnd) until piece measures 4½ in. (11.4cm) from beg. Place five more stitch markers evenly around (every 19 sts).

CROWN

Dec rnd: [Ssk, k to marker] six times. (6 sts decreased)

K 1 rnd.

Rep last 2 rnds ten more times. [48 sts]

Switch to dpns when there are too few sts for the circular needle.

Rep dec rnd every rnd until 6 sts rem. [K2tog, k1] twice. [4 sts]

Do not cut yarn.

TOPKNOT

Slip all sts onto one needle. *Slide work to right end of needle, k4; rep from * until cord measures 3½ in. (8.9cm) long. Cut the yarn and draw it through rem sts.

FINISHING

Tie a topknot with an overhand knot. Using the yarn end, tack it, end in place, to the underside of the knot. Lightly dampen the beret, and pull it over a 10-in. (25.4cm) dinner plate; allow it to dry thoroughly.

TIP
It is especially important to do a gauge swatch because this is a fitted project.

The topknot completes the swirl of a beret. For a trendier look, top the beret with a pompom in a complementary color.

Style Variation

The featured beret is so versatile that it can be dressed up or dressed down. Here, it is paired with a casual jean jacket and a turtleneck. The soft camel color of the beret and the hunter green of the sweater look great together.

three-strand
necklace

accents the neck in delicate beads

You will be making three different necklaces, which can be worn together—wrapped, tied, knotted—or alone. They go with practically everything from silk to denim. They can even be belted. This multi-layered look is definitely in style, and the white color and pearl adornments pull the look together.

SKILL LEVEL

Basic

MEASUREMENTS

- Finished lengths:
  Necklace #1: approx. 82" (208cm)
  Necklace #2: approx. 32" (81.2cm)
  Necklace #3: approx. 64" (162.5cm)

MATERIALS

- 163 yds. (150m) medium-weight rayon/polyster blend {one ball Patons "Katrina" [3½ oz. (100g)], #10005 white} (A)
- 153 yds. (140m) fine-weight nylon {one ball Katia "Sevilla" [1¾ oz. (50g)], #01 white} (B)
- 95 yds. (87m) bulky-weight rayon/cotton/nylon blend {one ball Katia "Ola" [1¾ oz. (50g)], #03 off-white} (C)
- 1 US 5 (3.75mm) and 1 US 9 (5.5mm) 24" (60cm) circular needle
- Sewing needle (to fit through all bead sizes)
- One skein DMC 6-strand embroidery floss, B5200 white
- Faux-pearl beads:
  80 round white, 10mm
  30 round cream, 10mm
  30 freshwater cream, 7mm
  150 round cream, 4mm

NECKLACE #1

With US 9 (5.5mm) needle and A and B held tog, cast on 350 sts. Work two rows st st (k on RS, p on WS). BO k-wise.

FINISHING

St st will curl to form a tube with the p side on the outside.

Using a needle and one strand of embroidery floss, attach the 10mm white pearls randomly along RS of the necklace, tying knots on the inside of the tube. Sew cast-on and bound-off edges together to close the tube if desired.

NECKLACE #2

Using US 5 (3.75mm) needles and one strand B, cast on 200 sts.
Row 1: *K1, p1; rep from * acrs. BO k-wise.

FINISHING

Using one strand of the embroidery floss, cut a 6-in. (15.2cm) length for each 10mm cream pearl. With the needle, thread a pearl onto the floss, and slide it to the center; tie the two ends in knots for 1 in. (2.54cm). Attach them by knotting the ends onto the necklace evenly along the entire

length and weaving in the ends. If desired, sew pearls onto the yarn tails at either end.

NECKLACE #3

Note: No knitting is involved. Cut a 12-in. (366cm) length of C.

FINISHING

Use a strand of embroidery floss and 4mm pearls to sew clusters of 3-5 pearls along the length of the ribbon with a running st between each cluster; pull the floss to gather the ribbon to 2 in. (5cm). Secure clusters with a backstitch. Sew larger clusters with 7mm and 4mm pearls.

> **TIP**
> When sewing with beads, waxing the thread will simplify beading.

GAUGE

- Necklace #1: 17 sts to 4" (10cm) measured over St st on US 9 (5.5mm) needles (or size to obtain gauge).
- Necklace #2: 25 sts to 4" (10cm) measured over k1, p1 rib on US 5 (3.75mm) needles (or size to obtain gauge).

ABBREVIATIONS
See page 82.

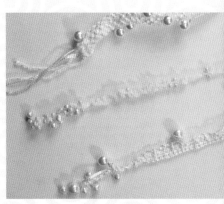

A trio of knitted strands are accented with lustrous pearls

Style Variation

The strands of the necklace are fun to wear as a belt whether together or singly. Wear the thicker, rope-style belt with trousers in a contrasting color. Or for a subtle look, wear one narrow strand at the waist of a long dress or skirt in white.

ruffled
scarf

for a pretty feminine look

Corkscrew, spiral, and ruffled are appropriate adjectives to describe this scarf. Its extra-long quality makes it quite versatile. Swirl it around your neck a few or many times so that the knitted fabric collects in soft coils around your neck. Or combine it with another slender knitted scarf in a similar colorway for a sophisticated layered look.

SKILL LEVEL
Basic

MEASUREMENTS
- Length: 55" (140cm), along the cast-on edge
- Width: 3" (7.6cm)

MATERIALS
- 110 yds. (102m) medium-weight cotton/nylon blend {one ball Berroco "Zen" [1¾ oz. (50g)], #8222 kimchi}
- 88 yds. (80.5m) medium-weight rayon {one ball Prism "Bon Bon" [2 oz. (56.7g)], #502 celery}
- 153 yds. (140m) fine-weight nylon {1 ball Katia "Sevilla" [1¾ oz. (50g)], #lime green}
- One US 10 (6mm) 36" (91.4cm) circular needle
- Tapestry needle

GAUGE
16 sts to 4" (10cm) measured over st st using US 10 (6mm) needle (or size to obtain gauge).

ABBREVIATIONS
See page 82.

SCARF

With A and C held tog, cast on 110 sts.

Drop A and C.

Row 1: WS. With B, p.

Row 2: With C, kfb of each st acrs. [220 sts]

Row 3: With C, p.

Row 4: With A, k.

Row 5: With B, k.

Row 6: With B, p.

Row 7: With C, kfb of each st acrs. [440 sts]

Row 8: With C, p.

Rows 9 and 10: With A, k.

BO P-wise with A.

TIP

Use a long circular needle to accommodate the large number of stitches.

When changing yarns, leave 6-in. (15.2cm) tails to use as fringe.

Style Variation

The ruffled scarf is a versatile accessory that is easy to make and perfect to wear no matter what the season. Of course, you can wear it as an indoor or out-door scarf. Lightweight and drapey, the scarf can be worn in place of a necklace. Wrap it casually around your neck so that one long end drapes down. Or wear the scarf as a frilly counterpoint to a strapless dress. Drape it casually at the neck of a softly structured blouse in a similar colorway, or use it in a similar way with a silk blazer in a contrasting color. To achieve the multi-layered look, pair it with another scarf (as shown in the photo). When the second scarf is in a similar color, the scarves will tell a texture story. Add a long beaded necklace for a fin-ishing touch that adds sparkle.

extra-long flirty scarf

with pom-poms

Banish the winter blahs by wrapping yourself in this cheery, ultra-warm scarf. Everything about it is fun! The bright colors, chunkiness, and pom-poms make it irresistible. And because it gradually narrows—becoming thinnest in the middle—you can coil it around your neck without that bulky look or feel.

SKILL LEVEL
Basic

MEASUREMENTS (Post-felting)
- Length: Approx. 84" (213.5cm)
- Width: Approx. 11" (28cm), at the ends, 4¼" (11cm) at the center

MATERIALS
- 660 yds. (600m) superbulky wool/acrylic blend {12 balls Lion Brand "Landscapes" [1¾ oz. (50g)], #280 raspberry patch} (A)
- 153 yds. (140m) each, two colors bulky wool/acrylic blend {one ball each, Lion Brand "Wool-Ease Chunky" [5 oz. (140g)], #140 deep rose (B) and #133 pumpkin (C)}
- Pair US 17 (12mm) needles
- Row counter
- Sewing needle and matching thread
- For felting: washer, measuring tape, mesh bag, laundry detergent, lint-free towel

ABBREVIATIONS
See page 82.

GAUGE
7 sts and 7.5 rows to 4" (10cm) measured over 3x1 Rib st, pre-felting
7 sts and 7.5 rows to 4" (10cm) measured over k3, p1 rib with two strands A held tog on US 17 (12mm) needles, pre-felting (or size to obtain gauge).

SCARF

With US 17 (1mm) needles and two strands A held tog, cast on 23 sts.

Row 1 (RS): (K3, p1) five times, k3.

Row 2: (P3, k1) five times, p3.

Rows 3-36: Rep rows 1-2.

Rows 37, 45, 53, 61, 69 and 77 (dec): Ssk, rib to the last 2 sts, k2tog. [11 sts. after row 77]

Rows 38-44, 46-52, 54-60, 62-68, 69-76 and 78-140: Rib as established.

Rows 141, 149, 157, 165, 173 and 181 (inc): Kfb, rib to the last st, kfb. [23 sts. after row 181]

Rows 142-148, 150-156, 158-164, 166-172, and 174-180: Rib as established, incorporating the increased sts into the rib pattern.

Row 182: Rep row 2.

Rows 183-214: Rep rows 1-2.

Row 215: Rep row 1.

FINISHING

Make 10 pom-poms* using B and C as foll: four 3-in. (7.6cm); six 2-in. (5.1cm). Make 10 braids for pom-poms as foll:

1. Cut four 12-in. (30.4cm) and six 10-in. (25.4cm) lengths of both B and C.

2. With one strand of each color, attach fringes. (See diagram.)

3. There will be four ends. Holding two ends together as one, braid the long fringes to 3 in. (7.6cm), and the shorter fringes to 2 in. (5.1cm); then knot the end.

4. Sew the short braids to the small pom-poms and the long braids to the large pom-poms.

* For detailed directions, see page 21.

((TIP))

Because you will be increasing and decreasing stitches on the outer edges of the scarf, maintain the 3/1 Rib with the additional stitches. Keep an eye on the pattern development so if you make a mistake, you'll catch it early. Using a row counter is a must for this project.

Placing the Pom-poms

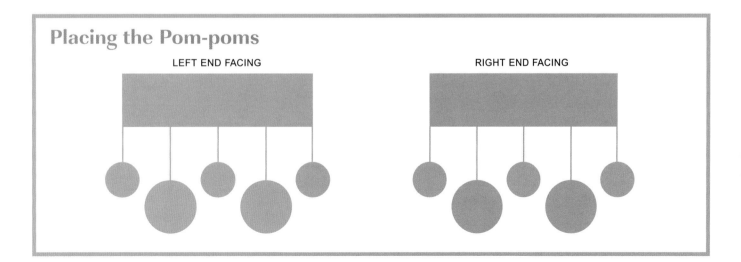

LEFT END FACING

RIGHT END FACING

Scarf Diagram

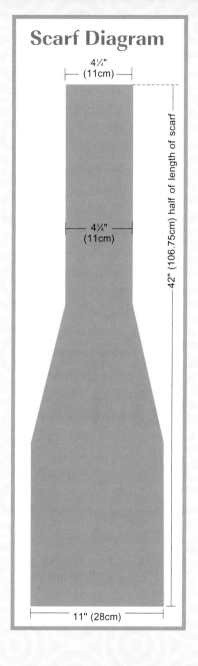

4¼" (11cm)

4¼" (11cm)

42" (106.75cm) half of length of scarf

11" (28cm)

Style Variations

There is an infinite number of ways to wear this extra-long scarf. Experiment with a wrap that suits you.

he versatility of this scarf is one of its many appealing aspects. Because the scarf is so long, it is easy to wrap in a fun variety of ways. It can be wrapped once around the neck so that the lengths fall below a pretty hemline. Or it can be wrapped twice around the neck so that the pom-poms come above the waist. Or simply fold the scarf in half, lay it around your neck, and thread the ends into the loop, allowing the bouncy pom-poms to swing below the waist. Another fun way to wear the scarf is to wrap it around and around your-neck until the pom-poms collect in a colorful cascade at your throat.

The Easy Way To Make a Pom-pom

The signature pom-poms on this scarf create colorful movement when the scarf is worn.

1. Wind yarn around a credit card 30 times. Slip the skein off of the card. Wind and knot a length of yarn around the skein to secure it. Repeat to make three more pom-poms.

2. Flatten and stack two pom-poms, matching their centers. Use a tapestry needle threaded with yarn to sew them together at their centers.

3. Stand the sewn pom-poms upright. Lay a third skein on top and sew it to the pair at their centers. Repeat to add a pom-pom to the other side.

4. Cut through all the yarn loops, and trim the yarn to form an even ball shape, using scissors.

coral and gray
cowl
neck

casual elegance in three styles

Y ou'll love the colors and textures of this smart muffler-style cowl. The gray cashmere-blend yarn and coral gossamer mohair produce a garment that feels as yummy as it looks. It can be worn in a variety of ways, including as a form-fitting bustier, depending upon your mood.

SKILL LEVEL
Intermediate

SIZES
S/M/L/XL

MEASUREMENTS
■ Length (including borders): 16/16/17.5/17.7" (40.6/40.6/44.5/44.5cm)
■ Width (across top edge): 26/28¾/31½/34¼" (66/73/80/87cm)

MATERIALS
■ 168 (252, 336, 336) yds. [154 (231, 308, 308)m] medium-weight cashmere or cashmere blend {two [three, four, four] balls Lion Brand "Lion Cashmere Blend" [1¼ oz. (40g)], #149 charcoal} (A)
■ 275 yds. (250m) superfine mohair blend {one ball Feza "Kid Mohair" [0.88 oz. (25g)], #203 coral} (B)
■ Pair each of US 7 (4.5mm), US 10 (6mm), US 11 (8mm), US 13 (9mm), US 15 (10mm), and US 17 (12mm) needles
■ Cable needle
■ One C/2 (2.5mm) crochet hook
■ Nine ⅝-in. buttons, 16mm
■ Tapestry needle
■ Sewing needle and thread to match

SPECIAL STITCHES

SHADOW CABLE STITCH

(Multiple of 8 sts + 2)

Cable 4 Back (C4B; uses 4 consecutive sts): Slip next 2 sts onto the CN and hold them in back of the work. K2 from the LN, then k2 from the CN.

Cable 4 Front (C4F; uses 4 consecutive sts): Slip the next 2 sts onto the CN and hold them in front of the work. K2 from the LN, then k2 from CN.

Rows 1 and 5 (RS): K.
Row 2 and all even-numbered rows: P.
Row 3: K1, *C4B, k4; rep from * to last st, k1.
Row 7: K5, *C4F, k4; rep from * to last 5 sts, C4F, k1.
Row 8: P.
Rep rows 1-8 for patt.

COWL

Follow the directions for small bustier.

BUSTIER

With US 11 (7mm) needles and A, cast on 74 (82, 90, 98) sts.
Rows 1 and 3: K.

Row 2: P. Add 2 strands B.
Rows 4 and 6: P.
Row 5: K.
Row 7: P.
Row 8: K. Drop both strands B.
Rows 9-40: Shadow cable.
Change to US 13 (9mm) needles.
Rows 41-48 (56): Shadow cable. Add 2 strands B and change to US 17 (12mm) needles.
Row 49 (57): K2, *p2, k2; rep from * to end.
Row 50 (58): P2, *k2, p2; rep from * to end.
Rows 51-55 (59-63): Rep rows 49-50 twice, and row 49 once more. BO in patt.

UPPER BORDER

With RS facing, using US 10 (6mm) needles and 2 strands B held tog, working in back loop only, pick up 74 (82, 90, 98) sts across bound-off edge.
Row 1 (WS): P.
Row 2: K.
Row 3: Change to US 13 (9mm) needles and p.
Row 4: Change to US 15 (10mm) needles and k.
Row 5: Change to US 17 (12mm) needles and p.
Row 6: K.

Row 7: P.
BO loosely k-wise.

LOWER BORDER

With RS facing, using the US 7 (4.5mm) needles and 2 strands B held tog, pick up 74 (82, 90, 98) sts across the cast-on edge.
Row 1 (WS): P.
Row 2: Change to US 10 (6mm) needles and k.
Row 3: Change to US 13 (9mm) needles and p.
Row 4: Change to US 15 (10mm) needles and k.
Row 5: Change to US 17 (12mm) needles and p.
BO loosely k-wise.

FINISHING

Block the cowl lightly to the measurements. Fold the bound-off edge of the lower border to the RS of the cast-on edge, and slip stitch it in place using a sewing needle and thread. Sew buttons along the left front edge, beginning and ending ¼ in. (0.63cm) from the end of the main body.
Button loops: Using a crochet hook and A, make nine 2.5-in.-long (6.25cm). Using yarn ends or a sewing needle and thread, attach the loops to the right front edge opposite buttons.

GAUGE

13 sts and 20 rows to 4 in. (10cm) measured over shadow cable stitch using US 11 (7mm) needles 13 sts and 20 rows to 4 in. (10cm) measured over shadow cable st on US 11 (7mm) needles (or size to obtain gauge).

ABBREVIATIONS

See page 82.

Wearing Styles

■ *A loose turtleneck*
■ *A tucked-in collar*

The Bustier

Perfect when paired with a lightweight V-neck sweater or shell, this bustier adds a touch of glamour that will take you from the office to a dinner in town without first stopping home to change. Fitted over another garment, the bustier buttons down the center and fits snugly on the body. Soft coral mohair forms the pretty border on the top edge, and gentle cables on the gray bodice lead the eye to the narrow salmon ruffle just touching the hips.

TIP

When the cowl is worn
as a bustier,
the buttons are featured,
so it's a good idea
to have the yarns with you
when selecting them.
In this project,
buttons are as important
as the yarn.

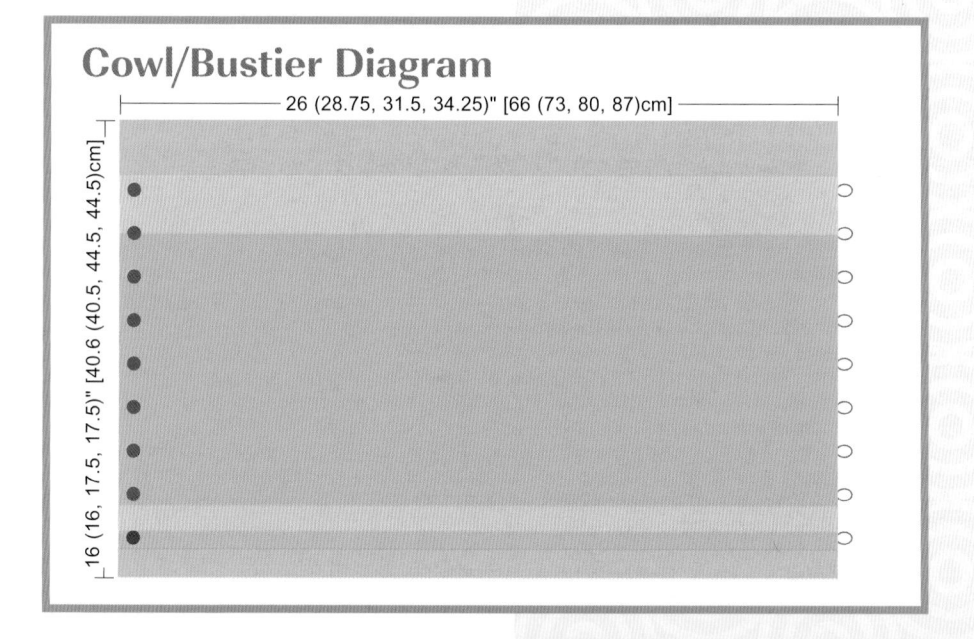

Cowl/Bustier Diagram

26 (28.75, 31.5, 34.25)" [66 (73, 80, 87)cm]

16 (16, 17.5, 17.5)" [40.6 (40.5, 44.5, 44.5)cm]

The Finishing instructions on page 23 direct you to use a crochet hook to make a chain for the button loops. If you don't know how to do that, it's not a problem. Here are some alternative methods to make loops. The first method involves casting on and binding off. The next two involve braiding and using ribbon.

TO KNIT THE BUTTON LOOPS

1. With a single strand of the cashmere blend yarn and very small needles, such as US 2 (2.75mm) or 3 (3.25mm), cast on approximately 10 stitches.
2. Don't knit any rows; simply bind off all stitches. (Don't knot the end so you can reuse the yarn.)
3. Measure the strip. If it is less than 2½ in. (6.4cm) long, cast on 2 or 3 more stitches [if it is longer than 2½ in. (6.4cm) long, cast on 2 or 3 fewer stitches] and repeat Step 2. Keep at this until you get the correct length.
4. Make eight more identical button loops.

TO BRAID THE BUTTON LOOPS

1. Cut 27 pieces [about 2¾ in. (7cm)] of the cashmere blend yarn.
2. Using three pieces for each braid, make nine of them. Use matching thread to tie off the ends. If desired, place a small dot of fabric glue on the tied-off areas.

A NON-BUTTON ALTERNATIVE

Use a tapestry needle and matching velvet or satin ribbon (thin) to lace up the garment. Make sure you purchase enough ribbon so that you can put the garment on and take it off without having to undo too much lacing. Tie the excess ribbon in a bow at the top or bottom of the bustier. If you don't like the bow, tuck the excess ribbon under the garment.

The rich texture of the gray yarn is highlighted by the tinge of soft salmon luster thrown off by the cast-metal buttons in aged copper. Coordinating all of the design elements makes good design sense.

TIP

Baste loops in place, try with buttons, make adjustments if needed; then sew securely.

―――――

The mohair yarn is delicate and should be knit loosely so that it will stretch. Bind off loosely!

muffler
with fur
pom-poms

*rich color and soft –
as-a-cloud feel*

Wearing a muffler indoors may be a surprising idea, but it isn't new. Pairing a scarf and a dress makes sense, especially in the colder months when you want to look elegant but you want to be warm. Here, a narrow cowl-style scarf accented with a jumble of fur pom-poms looks great with the little jacket and formal dress.

SKILL LEVEL
Basic

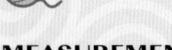

MEASUREMENTS
- Length: 25" (63.5cm), before finishing
- Width: 7¼" (18.4cm), before finishing

MATERIALS
- 153 yds. (140m) bulky-weight acrylic/wool blend {one ball Lion Brand "Wool-Ease Chunky" [5 oz. (14g)], #135 spice}
- Pair US 10.5 (6.5mm) needles
- 20 3" (7.6cm) fur pom-poms
- Tapestry needle
- Sewing needle and matching thread
- One K-10.5 (6.5mm) crochet hook
- Velcro strip for closure

GAUGE
11 sts and 13 rows to 4" (10cm) measured over k2, p2 rib on US 10.5 (6.5mm) needles (or size to obtain gauge).

ABBREVIATIONS
See page 82.

MUFFLER

Cast on 20 sts.

Row 1: RS. *K2, p2; rep from * to end of row.

Rep row 1 until muffler measures 25 in. (63.5cm).

BO in pattern.

FINISHING

1. Using a sewing needle and matching thread, attach ten pom-poms evenly along each long edge of the muffler.
2. Fold the muffler lengthwise, so one edge is 2 in. (5cm) above the other, and sew it in place.
3. Sew the side openings closed.
4. Using a crochet hook, make two 15 in. (38.1cm) chains for ties. Attach one to each end of the muffler at the fold.

⸨TIP⸩
Buy a scarf made entirely of pom-poms. Connected by a long cord, the pom-poms can be snipped off, one at a time, and sewn to your scarf.

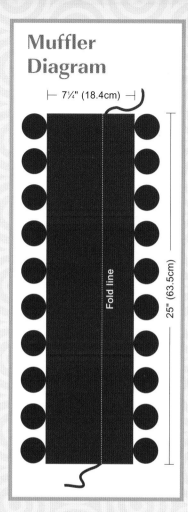

Muffler Diagram

⊢ 7¼" (18.4cm) ⊣

Fold line

25" (63.5cm)

Style Variation

For a bit of the rock & roll style, sew white pom-poms to the edge of a black scarf, adding crocheted ties to secure the ends of the scarf.

chenille
collar

office to evening

in one easy

accessory

SKILL LEVEL
Basic

MEASUREMENTS
- Length: approx. 32" (81.3cm)
- Width: approx. 5½" (14cm)

MATERIALS
- 100 yds. (91m) superbulky acrylic/rayon blend {Lion Brand "Chenille Thick & Quick [3½ oz. (99g)], #146 dark purple}
- Pair US 11 (8mm) needles
- Tapestry needle

GAUGE
8 sts and 14 rows to 4" (10cm) measured over st st on US 11 (8mm) needles (or size to obtain gauge).

ABBREVIATIONS
See page 82.

Jazz up a sweater coat or jacket by attaching this soft, warm, and colorful collar. You can't help feeling regal in chenille and royal purple! Because this project is done in stockinette stitch on fairly large needles, it knits up quickly. The character of the knitted fabric is somewhat drapey, but this is not a problem. The collar is small enough to maintain its structure, especially when it is laid over

a structured coat or jacket that supports the lines of the knitted piece.

Add your favorite pin, and you're all set for an evening out.

COLLAR

Cast on 2 sts.
Row 1 (WS): P.
Row 2: K1, kfb, k acrs.
Rows 3-20: Rep rows 1-2. [11 sts.
after row 20]
Rows 21-93: St st.
Row 94: K1, k2tog, k acrs.
Row 95: P.
Rows 96-111: Rep rows 92-93.
[2 sts. after row 111]
BO k-wise.

This lush purple collar was inspired by Lion Brand Yarn Company's Pattern #40431 ("Capelet") design. Originally shaped like a cape collar, this design was altered so that the collar can be worn over a coat or jacket that has a lapel. The idea behind the change was based on looking for a resourceful way to revive interest in last season's wardrobe. By adding a colorful collar in a contrasting color, the coat appears new and stylish. The collar might also be made in a black chenille, lending some luxury to an everyday black coat. For a casual look, replace the chenille with a different type of super-bulky yarn.

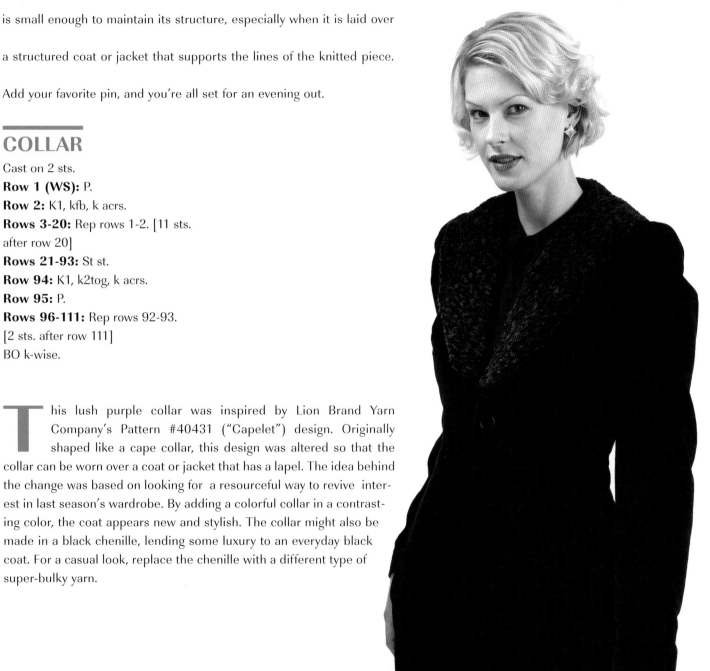

⟨TIP⟩
Save yarn labels
because they contain
important
care instructions.

Style Variation
Instead of laying the collar flat, wrap the collar around your neck so that it looks like a cowl. Secure the overlap on the inside with a safety pin or on the outside with a pretty brooch.

bronze collar with pin accent

a little glitz for party glamour

Transform your basic sheath into party attire with this bronze metallic collar—a necklace, really. Leave the ties hanging loosely so that the collar remains slightly open. Or connect the ties to give the impression of a lustrous mock turtleneck. For more style, add the petaled flower to one side of the collar.

SKILL LEVEL

Basic

MEASUREMENTS

- Collar length: 7" (17.8cm)
- Collar width: 14" (35.6cm) at neck edge, 19" (48.3cm) at lower edge
- Flower: approx. 4½" (11.4cm) in diameter

MATERIALS

- Collar:
  - 115 yds. (105m) medium-weight metallic acrylic/polyester blend {one skein Lion Brand "Glitterspun" [1¾ oz. (50g)], #135 bronze} (A)
  - 153 yds. (140m) fine-weight nylon {one ball Katia "Sevilla" [1¾ oz. (50g)], #17 brown} (B)
  - Pair each US 10 (6mm), US 13 (9mm), US 15 (10mm), US 17 (12mm), US 19 (15mm) needles
- Flower:
  - Leftover A and B yarn from collar
  - 104 yds. (95m) lightweight cotton/wool/Lycra blend {one ball Heirloom "Breeze" [1¾ oz. (50g)], #001 white} (C)
  - 122 yds. (110m) bulky suede-like polyester {one skein Lion Brand "Suede" [3 oz. (85g)], #126 coffee} (D)
  - 75 yds (70m) eyelash {one ball Knitting Fever "Flutter"

BRONZE COLLAR

With US 10 (6mm) needles and A and B held tog, cast on 60 sts.

Rows 1-12: *K2, p2; rep from * to end.

Change to US 13 (9mm) needles.

Rows 13 and 14: Rep row 1.

Change to US 15 (10mm) needles.

Rows 15 and 16: Rep row 1.

Change to US 17 (12mm) needles.

Rows 17 and 18: Rep row 1.

Change to US 19 (15mm) needles.

Rows 19-22: Rep row 1.

BO in patt.

FINISHING

Ties

1. Cut 12 22-in. (55.9cm) lengths each of A and B.
2. Mark six points evenly along each side edge for the ties.
3. Thread one strand each of A and B through each point; pull the yarn halfway through, and tie a double knot to secure it. You now have four 11-in. (27.9cm) strands.
4. Holding two of the strands as one, braid the strands.
5. Tie the ends in an overhand knot to secure them.

PIN

Flower

With a beading needle and beading thread, string the entire strand of seed beads.

With US 3 (3.25mm) needles and C, cast on 100 sts.

Row 1 (RS): K.

Change to US 5 (3.75mm) needles.

Row 2: P.

Drop C and pick up D.

Row 3: K.

Drop D and pick up A.

Row 4: P.

Drop A and pick up C.

Row 5: K.

Join the strand of seed beads.

Row 6: With C and the seed beads, p.

Drop the strand of seed beads, carefully securing the ends.

Row 7: With C, k.

Drop C and pick up A.

Row 8: P.

Drop A and pick up D.

Row 9: K.

Drop D and pick up C and E.

Row 10: With C and E, p.

Drop C and pick up A.

Row 11: With E and A, k.

Drop E.

Row 12: With A, p.

BO k-wise.

FINISHING

1. With A and B tog, make one 1¼-in. (3.18cm) pom-pom.
2. With B, make two 1½-in. (3.8cm) tassels; with D, make one 1½-in. (3.8cm) tassel; using 10 lengths of yarn per tassel.
3. Cut off a piece of A slightly longer than the length of the petal. Thread it onto the tapestry needle, and baste across the petal approx ¼" (0.64cm) from the bound off edge.
4. Pull on the ends of A to gather, and form into a three-petal shape that you like, tacking into place on WS with sewing needle and thread.
5. Attach the tassels to the RS center of the flower.
6. Attach the pom-pom to the RS center of the flower.
7. Arrange the tassel ends around the pom-pom, and snip them to various lengths until you like the way your flower looks.
8. Sew the pin to the back of the flower.

TIP

After cutting metallic yarn, apply a small amount of fray preventative to the ends.

[¾ oz. (20g)], #01 white} (E)

- 110 yds. (102m) medium-weight cotton/nylon blend {one ball Berroco "Zen" [1¾ oz. (50g)], #8222 kimchi} (F)
- Pair each US 3 (3.25mm), US 5 (3.75mm) needles
- Sewing needle and matching threads
- Tapestry needle
- Pin back
- Beading needle
- 10g beading string
- Beads:
  - One strand seed beads, bronze
  - 10 freshwater pearls 10mm, bronze
  - Five round 2mm, gold
  - Five round 2.5mm, gold
  - 5 round 6mm, gold

GAUGE

17 sts and 22 rows to 4" (10cm) measured over k2, p2 rib on US 10 (6mm) needles (or size to obtain gauge).

ABBREVIATIONS

See page 82.

VINES & LEAVES

Small (medium) bobble leaves: Make four (six) each, measuring ¾ in. (1.9cm) [1 in. (2.5cm)]

With US 3 (3.25mm) needles and F, make a slip knot, and place it on needle.

Row 1 (WS): (K1, p1, k1, p1, k1) all in one st. [5 sts]

Tug on the tail to tighten the slip knot.

Rows 2 and 4: K.

Row 3: P.

MEDIUM ONLY: Rep rows 3 and 4 once more.

Row 5: P1, p3tog, p1. [3 sts]

Row 6: Sk2p. [1 st]

Cut the yarn, leaving a long tail for sewing. Fasten it off by drawing the tail through the last st.

FINISHING

1. With F, make five braided vines of varying lengths.
2. Place two bobble leaves with WS together, inserting one end of braided vine between them.
3. Sew around bobble leaves, being sure to secure vine in place.
4. Sew a freshwater pearl to the front and the back of each leaf.
5. String three gold beads tog, and sew them to the leaf tips. (See diagram.)
6. Sew the ends of the vines tog, and attach them to back of the flower.

TIP

Even though you are sewing the strands to the back of the flower, use fabric glue as reinforcement.

Style Variation

Try adding fringe or very small beaded pom-poms (dangling or sewn to the edge) to the lower edge of the collar. Choose bronze for a subtle look. The small details will highlight the curvey silhouette of the collar and add glamor to the bodice.

HELPFUL HINTS

Treat the collar carefully because it snags easily.

Stringing seed beads can be extremely tedious unless you use a technique I discovered after hours of asking myself, "Why am I doing this again?" Place the seed beads in a shallow, preferably rectangular, container, and tip it so that the beads collect along one of the long sides. After threading the needle (not forgetting to wax the thread), hold it horizontally, and swipe it—not too fast—through the center of the collected beads, gradually tipping the needle up so that the beads will stay on the needle. When you've caught about 1 inch (2.54cm) or so of beads, slide them onto the thread, and continue "fishing."

Keeping the yarn and bead strands together, p gently. Keep the bead strand fairly taut along the yarn strand—but not tight—so that you do not break it.

Note: small projects like the flower require minimal amounts of yarn, so go through your yarn stash before purchasing more. Use your imagination as you go through your collection.

Consider mixing colors not usually found in nature to achieve a high-style look. Consider the yarn color first; then coordinate the yarn for the flower. A flower in chartreuse, for example, would look striking against a collar made in shimmering cobalt blue. And a metallic silver flower would dazzle a collar made in a white metallic yarn.

TIP
Remember to be careful when removing the pin from the collar; once pulled out of place, this yarn is very hard to put back!

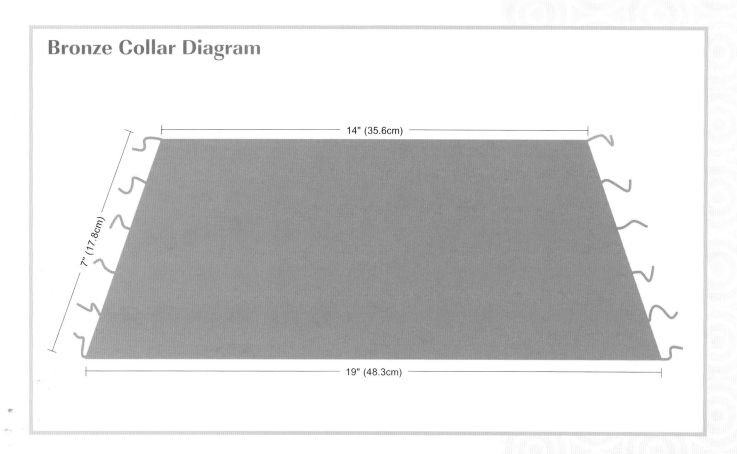

Bronze Collar Diagram

14" (35.6cm)

7" (17.8cm)

19" (48.3cm)

elegant black
cuff

display a
favorite pin

E legant and understated, this knitted cuff is perfect for casual or dressy outfits. Great with a pearl-gray sweater with long sleeves or with a flowing cami, the cuff is an attractive counterpoint. Worked in garter stitch on small needles, subtle ridges blend into a soft layer of yarn at the wrist. Jet-black beads add some glint and shine, and an antique cameo establishes the cuff's classic style.

SKILL LEVEL
Basic

MEASUREMENTS
- Length: 7.7" (19.1cm)
- Width: 3" (7.6cm)

MATERIALS
- 158 yds. (144m) medium-weight wool {one ball Lion Brand "Lion Wool" [3 oz. (85g)], #153 black}
- Pair US 6 (4mm) needles
- Cameo pin (or pin of your choice)
- 55 round black beads, 5mm
- Black thread
- Tapestry needle
- Sewing needle (must fit through beads)

GAUGE
20 sts and 40 rows to 4" (10cm) measured over garter stitch on US 6 (4mm) needles (or size to obtain gauge).

ABBREVIATIONS
See page 82.

CUFF

Cast on 30 sts.
K every row until the cuff measures
3 in. (7.6cm).
BO k-wise.

OVERLAP

Pick up 15 sts across one short end of
the cuff.
K every row for 1 in. (2.5cm) or to the
desired length.
BO k-wise.

FINISHING

With a tapestry needle and thread,
make a small loop at each end of the
bind-off row of overlap. The hole
should be just large enough for a bead
to squeeze through it.

CLOSURES

1. Thread a darning needle with yarn,
   knotting the end.
2. Insert the needle from the WS to
   the RS at one end of the bind-off
   row of overlap, burying the knot
   between the stitches.
3. Reinsert the needle into the bind-
   off row, approximately ¼ in.
   (0.64cm) from the first insertion.

4. Pull the yarn until a ⅜-in. (1cm)
   diameter loop forms.
5. Use a buttonhole stitch to
   finish the loop.
6. Reinsert the needle into the
   first insertion point, and
   make small running stitches to the other end of the
   bind-off row.
7. Repeat steps 2–5 for the
   second loop.
8. Secure and weave in end
   on the WS.

With a sewing needle and thread, sew
beads evenly across the top and bottom edges of the cuff, ⅛ in. (0.32cm)
from the edge.

Center the cameo on the cuff
section. Sew evenly spaced
beads around it.

To close the cuff, place
the overlap over the end,
slipping the loops
around the beads at
the top and bottom
edges. Use other
sets of beads to
adjust the fit.

TIP

Adjust the width
of the bracelet
to complement
your pin.

Style Variation

*Try a variety of weights and
types of yarn for totally different
looks. A gorgeous button or
bead can also serve as the
bracelet's focal point.*

eyelash beaded cuff

a bit of stately fun for your wrist

Finding ways to use novelty yarns is easy when you decide to mix them with pretty buttons and unique beads. Here, a knitted cuff in purple and black is decorated with glistening glass beads with snowy centers. The oval button at the loop closure is an eye-catching detail that echoes the style of the cuff.

SKILL LEVEL
Intermediate

MEASUREMENTS
■ Length: 7" (17.8cm)
■ Width: 2" (5.1cm)

MATERIALS
■ 127 yds. (116m) medium-weight cotton {one ball Artfibers "Papyrus" [1¾ oz. (50g)], #014 purple} (A)
■ 153 yds. (140m) fine-weight nylon {one ball Katia "Sevilla" [1¾ oz. (50g)], #02 black} (B)
■ 80 yds. (74m) polyester eyelash {one ball Trendsetter "Eyelash" [0.7 oz. (20g)], #5 black} (C)
■ Pair US 7 (4.5mm) needles
■ 72 triangular clear-glass beads with white centers, 8mm
■ One ⅞" (2.22cm) oval button
■ Sewing needle and thread to match A

GAUGE
18 sts and 30 rows to 4" (10cm) measured over beaded garter stitch with A, B, and C held tog on US 7 (4.5mm) needles (or size to obtain gauge).

ABBREVIATIONS
See page 82.

SPECIAL STITCH

Beads over slip stitch (BOSS): Bring the yarn to the front of the work. Slide a bead up to the needle, holding it snugly against the needle; slip the next st p-wise, and bring the yarn to the back of work; and k the next st.

CUFF

String all the beads onto A (you will slide beads into place as needed, one at a time).

With US 7 (4.5mm) needles, and A, B, and C held together, cast on 9 sts.

Rows 1-3: K.

Row 4: K1, [BOSS] 4 times.

Row 5: K.

Row 6: K2, [BOSS] 3 times, k1.

Row 7: K.

Rep rows 4–7 until the bracelet is 6¾ in. (17.1cm) or ¼ in. (0.64cm) less than the desired length. Knit 2 rows. BO K-wise. Snip yarns, leaving 6-in. (15.2cm) tails.

FINISHING

Sew the button onto the RS of one end, ½ in. (1.27cm) from the edge.

Weave in the tails of B and C. Threaded with a 12-in. (30.4cm) length of A, insert a tapestry needle through the cuff at the base of the tail end of A; pull the

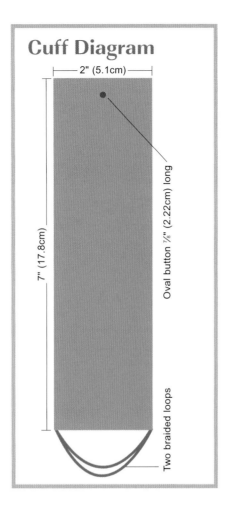

Cuff Diagram

2" (5.1cm)

7" (17.8cm)

Oval button ⅞" (2.22cm) long

Two braided loops

yarn halfway through so that there are 3 strands of A. Braid and secure the ends with a needle and thread. To form a double-button loop, slip the braid halfway through sts at the other corner and knot; then bring the end to the base of the braid, and sew it down securely.

Style Variation

For a summer look, choose yarns in mouth-watering colors like tropical orange and cherry red. Or make up the bracelet in saffron-colored yarn, pairing it with a richly colored halter top and flowing skirt in paprika. The bracelet knits up in so little time, you will want to make several for every season.

beaded cuff with beaded fringe

covered in crystals and bordered by beaded fringe

The metallic ribbon yarn looks great knitted on small needles in moss stitch; the result is a bronze mesh that forms a lush background for the beautiful crystal beads. As if the bracelet weren't elegant enough, delicate beaded fringe raises it to another level. You'll definitely feel fancy wearing this bracelet.

SKILL LEVEL
Basic

MEASUREMENTS
- Length: 7" (17.8cm), before fringe
- Width: 2" (5.1cm), after beading

MATERIALS
- 153 yds. (140m) fine-weight nylon {one ball Katia "Sevilla" [1¾ oz. (50g)], #17 brown}
- Pair US 5 (3.75mm) needles
- Four strands gold seed beads
- Two strands clear, crystal seed beads
- Approx. 60 bi-cone crystal beads in moss green, 5mm
- 300 bi-cone crystal beads in garnet, 5mm
- Approx. 160 bi-cone clear crystal beads, 5mm
- Three glass beads, 8mm dia.
- Clear filament thread
- Beading needle

GAUGE
24 sts to 4" (10cm) measured over moss stitch on US 5 (3.75mm) needles (or size to obtain gauge).

ABBREVIATIONS
See page 82.

CUFF

Cast on 14 sts.

Rows 1 and 2: *K1, p1; rep from * to end.

Rows 3 and 4: *P1, k1; rep from * to end.

Rep rows 1–4 to 7 in. (17.8cm) or desired length.

BO in patt.

BEADING INSTRUCTIONS

Refer to the beading diagram.

1. Thread a beading needle with a 12-in. (30.5cm) length of clear filament and knot one end.
2. Begin beading gold seed beads at one edge of the cuff. Bring the needle from the back to front of the cuff, picking up three gold seed beads.
3. Push the loaded needle to the back of the cuff, fitting the beads snugly against the knitted fabric.
4. Make 2 or 3 tiny backstitches to secure.

Repeat steps 2–4 until the cuff is fully decorated.

For added sparkle, apply a ¼-in.-wide (64cm) swath of crystal beads in moss green in a random pattern to the top and bottom edges or following the beading diagram. You can also add three lines of crystal beads in garnet across the top, middle, and bottom edges of the beaded band, spacing them at broad intervals or as desired.

FRINGE

1. Thread a beading needle with a 12-in. (30.5cm) length of clear filament, and knot one end.
2. Bring the needle up through the edge, a scant ⅛ in. (0.32cm) from the edge.
3. String on nine beads, alternating garnet and clear crystal beads.
4. At the bottom, string on a seed bead and re-insert the needle back through the entire strand, anchoring the strand using 2 or 3 backstitches at the knitted edge.
5. Poke the needle under the edge of the band, and come back up and out at a point ¼ in. (0.64cm) away from the previous strand.
6. String on five beads, alternating garnet and clear crystal beads.

Repeat steps 3–6 for each fringe set, working across the entire length of the cuff.

FINISHING

Closure beads

Sew three 8mm beads across one short edge for closure; one at each corner and one in the center.

Closure loops

(worked on the opposite edge)

1. Thread a darning needle with yarn, knotting the end.
2. Insert the needle from WS to RS at one end of the short edge, burying the knot between stitches.
3. Reinsert the needle into the edge, approx. ¼ in. (0.64cm) from the first insertion.
4. Pull the yarn until a loop forms, just large enough for the closure bead to squeeze through.
5. Use a buttonhole stitch to finish the loop.
6. Reinsert the needle into the first insertion point.
7. Make small running stitches to the center of the short edge, and repeat steps 2–6 for the second loop.
8. Make running stitches to the other end of of the short edge. Repeat steps 2–6 for the third loop.
9. Secure the end on the WS.

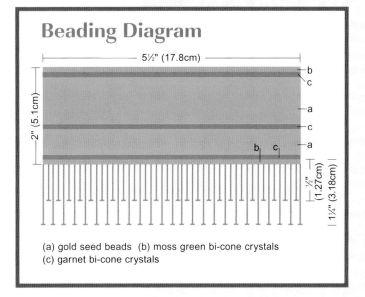

Beading Diagram

5½" (17.8cm) · 2" (5.1cm) · ½" (1.27cm) · ¼" (3.18cm) · 1¼"

b · c · a · c · a · b · c

(a) gold seed beads (b) moss green bi-cone crystals
(c) garnet bi-cone crystals

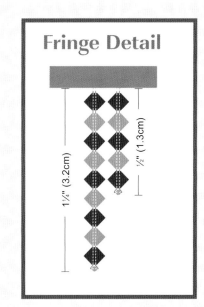

Fringe Detail

1¼" (3.2cm) · ½" (1.3cm)

mini shawl collar

with button

The soft, warm blend of lamb's wool and acrylic yarn gives this minishawl collar a cozy, practical feel, and the orange color adds contemporary elegance. A deceptively simple seed stitch, worked in superbulky yarn using fat needles, creates an elaborate texture. The shawl's construction is easy, too: fold over a long edge of an extra-wide knitted rectangle; overlap the ends; and secure them with a vintage button.

SKILL LEVEL
Basic

MEASUREMENTS
- Length: 41" (104.1cm)
- Width: 9" (48.3cm)

MATERIALS
- 459 yds. (420m) bulky acrylic/wool blend {three skeins Lion Brand "Wool-Ease Chunky" [5 oz. (140g)], #133 pumpkin}
- Pair US 10 (6mm) needles
- One black button, 4cm
- One round orange bead, 6mm (optional)
- Tapestry needle and thread
- Darning needle
- Large safety pins

GAUGE
9 sts and 15 rows to 4" (10cm) measured over seed stitch on US 10 (6mm) needles (or size to obtain gauge).

ABBREVIATIONS
See page 82.

Shawl Diagram

Fold line

4½" (11.4cm)

5½" (14cm)

19" (48.3cm)

41" (104.1cm)

SHAWL

Cast on 44 sts.

Row 1: RS. *K1, p1; rep from * to end.

Row 2: *P1, k1; rep from * to end. Rep rows 1 and 2 until piece measures 41 in. (104.1cm). BO in patt.

FINISHING

1. Lay the knitted fabric horizontally on a flat surface.
2. To create the collar, fold over a 5½-in.-wide (14cm) hem at the top edge, marking the fold line with safety pins.
3. Thread the darning needle with yarn, and using a running stitch, tack down the collar along the marked fold line, keeping the stitches hidden and removing the pins as you work.
4. Lay the shawl horizontally on a flat surface, WS up. Bring the ends together, overlapping the left edge over the right edge by 4½ in. (11.4cm).
5. Position the button on the right side of the collar. Then sew on the button adding a bead to conceal the holes, if desired.

CLOSURE

1. Thread a tapestry needle with yarn, knotting the end.
2. Insert the needle from WS to RS at the fold line of the left edge, burying the knot between stitches.
3. Reinsert the needle into the left edge, approximately 1¼ in. (3.2cm) from the first insertion.
4. Pull the yarn until a ¾-in.-diameter (1.9cm) loop forms.
5. Use a buttonhole stitch to finish the loop.

⟨TIP⟩

Fitting

The fit of the shawl is comfortably snug across the shoulders, with a jaunty overlap at the front that allows the points of the collar to be seen. To wear the minishawl closer and higher on the neck, increase the width of the overlap, moving the button accordingly to secure the shawl.

Sizing

Work in pattern until the fabric is long enough to surround your shoulders with the ends overlapping at the front by 4½ in. (11.4cm). You may need to purchase extra yarn for a larger size.

Style Variation

For a different look, wear the shawl lower in front, allowing the back to rise to the middle of the back and the overlapped collar to drop into a deep "V."

chunky
ponchette

the "goes-with-anything" staple

Because of the large needles and chunky yarn, you'll be done with this project in no time. Cropped and styled to be worn slightly off the shoulder, the ponchette works as well with a strapless dress as it does with a T-shirt and jeans. Combining two medium-weight yarns yields an extra-chunkiness and bold color that make this ponchette stylish and comfortable to wear anytime.

SKILL LEVEL
Intermediate

SIZES
S/M/L

MEASUREMENTS
- Length: 14 (14½, 15¼)" [35.6 (36.8, 38.7)cm]
- Width, neck edge: 14 (15¼, 16½)" [35.6 (38.7, 41.9)cm]
- Width, lower edge: 20 (23, 26)" [50.8 (58.4, 66)cm]

MATERIALS
- 330 (385, 440) yds. [300 (350, 500)cm] medium-weight acrylic/wool blend {six (seven, eight) balls Lion Brand "Landscapes" [1¾ oz. (50g)], #271 rose garden} (A)
- 396 yds. (360m) medium-weight acrylic/wool blend {two balls Lion Brand "Wool-Ease Worsted Weight" [3 oz. (85g)], in #139 dark rose heather} (B)
- Pair each US 13 (9mm) needles, US 17 (12mm) needles.
- Cable needle
- Tapestry needle
- Stitch markers

GAUGE
8 sts and 12 rows to 4" (10cm) measured over St st with A and B held tog on US 17 (12mm) needles (or size to obtain gauge).

ABBREVIATIONS
See page 82.

SPECIAL STITCHES

Cable 6 Back (C6B) (uses six consecutive stitches): Slip next 3 sts onto the CN and hold them in back of the work. K3 from the LN, then k3 from the CN.

PONCHETTE

(make two pieces)

With one strand each of A and B held tog using US 17 (12 mm) needles, cast on 46 sts.

Rows 1 and 5: RS. P4 (7, 11), *k6, p5, [k1, p1] twice, p1, k6, p2, [k1, p1] twice, p4, k6*, p4 (7, 11).

Rows 2 and 4: K4 (7, 11), *p6, k5, [p1, k1] twice, k1, p6, k2, [p1, k1] twice, k4, p6*, k4 (7, 11).

Row 3: P4 (7, 11), *C6B, p5, [k1, p1] twice, p1, C6B, p2, [k1, p1] twice, p4, C6B*, p4 (7, 11).

Row 6: K4 (7, 11), *p6, k5, [p1, k1] twice, k1, p6, k2, [p1, k1] twice, k4, p6*, k4 (7, 11).

Rows 7-14: Rep rows 1-6, then rows 1-2 once more.

Row 15: P1, p2tog, p1 (4, 8), rep row 3 from * to *, p1 (4, 8), p2tog, p1. [44 (50, 58) sts]

Rows 16-24: Rep rows 4-6 once, then rows 1-6 once, working p or k3 (6, 10) at beg and end of row instead of p or k4 (7, 11).

Row 25: P1, p2tog, p0 (3, 7), rep row 1 from * to *, p0 (3, 7), p2tog, p1. [42 (48, 56) sts]

Rows 26-30: Rep rows 2-6, working p or k2 (5, 9) at beg and end of row instead of p or k4 (7, 11).
Drop B and change to US 13 (9 mm) needles.

Rows 31-36: Rep rows 1-6, working p or k2 (5, 9) at beg and end of row instead of p or k4 (7, 11).

SIZE M ONLY:

Row 37: P1, p2tog, p2, rep row 6 from * to *, p2, p2tog, p1. [46 sts]

Row 38: Rep row 2, working k4 at beg and end of row instead of k7.

SIZE L ONLY:

Row 37: P1, p2tog, p3, p2tog, p1, rep row 1 from * to *, p1, p2tog, p3, p2tog, p1. [52 sts]

Row 38: Rep row 2, working k7 at beg and end of row instead of k11.

Row 39: P1, p2tog, p4, rep row 3 from * to *, p4, p2tog, p1. [50 sts]

Row 40: Rep row 4, working k6 at beg and end of row instead of k11.

NECKBAND

Pick up B and change to US 17 (12 mm) needles.

Row 1: RS. *P2, k2; rep from * to last 2 sts, p2.

Row 2: K2, *p2, k2; rep from * to end.

Rows 3-5: Rep rows 1-2 once, then row 1 once more.
BO loosely in patt.

FINISHING

Block both pieces to the same measurements. Join the side seams using B and a tapestry needle, working in the center of the edge stitches.

HELPFUL HINTS

I've found that I am less likely to inadvertently ignore a cable section if I define its boundaries with stitch markers. Unless otherwise noted, slip the markers onto the right needle as you come to them.

The knitted pattern is enhanced by the yarn in confetti-colors.

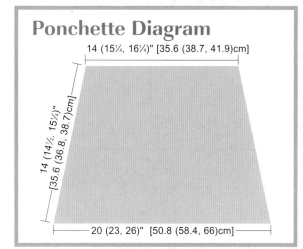

Ponchette Diagram

14 (15¼, 16¼)" [35.6 (38.7, 41.9)cm]

14 (14½, 15¼)" [35.6 (36.8, 38.7)cm]

20 (23, 26)" [50.8 (58.4, 66)cm]

lacy
shrug

with fur collar and cuffs

A shrug is one of the most versatile wardrobe pieces because it can be dressed up or down. Here, an open-weave stitch created an elegant fabric in a strawberry color. The knitted stitch was formed by pairing a suede yarn that has a subtle ombre effect with a nubby yarn. The faux fur collar was added separately, as were faux fur cuffs, lending glamour-girl appeal.

SKILL LEVEL Intermediate

SIZES S (M, L, XL)

MEASUREMENTS
- Length: 10 (11.5, 13, 15)" [25.4 (26.7, 27.9, 29.2)cm]
- Width of back opening: 20 (22, 24, 26)" [50.8 (55.9, 61, 66)cm]
- Wrist: 8 (8.75, 9.25, 10)" [20.3 (22.2, 23.5, 25.4)cm]

MATERIALS
- 240 (240, 240, 360) yds. [222 (222, 222, 333)m] bulky suede-like nylon {two (two, two, three) balls Berocco "Suede" [1¾ oz. (50g)], #3751 strawberry} (A)
- 163 yds. (150m) lightweight rayon/cotton/nylon blend {one ball Tahki Stacy Charles "Muse" [1¾ oz. (50g)], #14 red multi} (B)
- 61 yds. (55.8m) medium-weight rayon microfiber/wool blend {one ball Muench Yarns "Touch Me" [1¾ oz. (50g)], #3642 pink} (C)
- Pair each US 7 (4.5mm), US 10.5 (6.5mm), US 11 (8mm), US 13 (9mm), US 15 (10mm), US 17 (12mm), US 35 (19mm)
- Tapestry needle
- Stitch markers
- Optional: 18 (20, 22, 24)" [45.7 (50.8, 55.9, 61)cm] length of fur trim

GAUGE
12.5 sts and 16 rows to 4" (10cm)

STITCH PATTERN

Crocus bud stitch

(Multiple of 2 sts + 1)

Row 1 (RS): 1; *yo, k2; rep from * to end.

Row 2: P1, *p3, using the LN slip the 3rd st on the RN over the first 2 sts on the RN; rep from * to the end of row.

Row 3: *K2, yo; rep from * to the last st; k1.

Row 4: *P3; using the LN slip the 3rd st on the RN over the first 2 sts on the RN; rep from * to last st; p1.

Repeat Rows 1–4 for the patt.

SHRUG

With US 10.5 (6.5mm) needles and A, cast on 25 (27, 29, 31) sts.

Rows 1-24: Work in the crocus bud st patt.

Change to US 11 (8mm) needles.

Rows 25-28: Work in the crocus bud st patt.

Row 29 (inc): K1, pm, m1, work in the crocus bud st patt from * to the last st, m1, pm, k1. [27 (29, 31, 33) sts]

Rows 30-32, 34-36 and 38-48: Work in the st st to marker, sm, continue in the crocus bud st patt to the marker, sm, work in the st st to the end.

Rows 33 and 37 (inc): K1, m1, work in st st to the marker, sm, work in the crocus bud st patt from * to the marker, sm, work in st st to last st, m1, k1. [31 (33, 35, 37) sts after row 37]

Change to US 13 (9mm) needles.

Row 49 and 61 (inc): Rep row 33. [35 (37, 39, 41) sts. after row 61]

Rows 50-60 and 62-64: Work in st st to the marker, sm, work in the crocus bud st patt to the marker, sm, work in st st to the end.

Change to US 15 (10mm) needles, removing the markers.

Rows 65-68: *K1, p1; rep from * to last st, k1.

Change to US 17 (12mm) needles.

Row 69 (inc): Kfb, *p1, k1; rep from * to the last st, m1, kfb. [37 (39, 41, 43) sts]

Rows 70-72: *P1, k1; rep from * to the last st, p1.

Change to US 35 (19mm) needles.

Rows 73-84: Rep row 70.

Sizes M (L, XL) only: Rep row 70 for 2 (4, 6) in. [5.1 (10.2, 15.2)cm] more, ending after a WS row. (Note: place a marker at row 84 to keep track.)

Change to US 17 (12mm) needles.

Rows 85-88: Rep row 70.

Row 89 (dec): Ssk, *p1, k1; rep from * to the last 3 sts, p1, k2tog. [35 (37, 39, 41) sts]

Change to US 15 (10mm) needles.

Rows 90-92: *K1, p1; rep from * to the last st, k1.

Change to US 13 (9mm) needles.

Row 93: K5, pm, work in the crocus bud st patt to the last 5 sts, pm, k5.

Rows 94-96: Work in st st to the marker, sm, work in the crocus bud st patt to the marker, sm, work in st st to the end.

Row 97 (dec): Ssk, k3, sm, work in the crocus bud st patt to the marker, sm, k3, k2tog. [33 (35, 37, 39) sts]

Rows 98-108: Rep row 94.

Row 109 (dec): Ssk, k2, sm, work in the crocus bud st patt to marker, sm, k2, k2tog. [31 (33, 35, 37) sts]

Change to US 11 (8mm) needles.

Rows 110-120: Rep row 94.

Row 121 (dec): Ssk, k1, sm, work in the crocus bud st patt to the marker, sm, k1, k2tog. [29 (31, 33, 35) sts]

Rows 122-124: Rep row 94.

Row 125 (dec): Ssk, rm, work in crocus bud st patt to marker, rm, k2tog. [27 (29, 31, 33) sts]

Rows 125-128: Rep row 94.

Row 129 (dec): Ssk, *yo, k2; rep from * to the last 3 sts, yo, k1, k2tog. [25 (27, 29, 31) sts.]

Rows 130-132: Work in the crocus bud st patt.

Change to US 10.5 (6.5mm) needles.

Rows 133-156: Work in the crocus bud st patt.

BO k-wise.

(continued on next column)

measured over crocus bud st on US 10.5 (6.5mm) needles and A (or size to obtain gauge).

ABBREVIATIONS

See page 82.

WRIST TRIM

Using US 7 (4.5mm) needles and B, pick up 39 (43, 45, 49) sts evenly across cast-on edge.

Rows 1-5: *K1, p1; rep from * to last st, k1.

Drop B and join C, leaving a long tail for ties.

Row 6: P.

Row 7: K.

BO P-wise, leaving a long tail for ties.

FINISHING

1. Fold the garment in half lengthwise.

2. Sew the sleeve seams using a tapestry needle and A, leaving 2.5" (6.35cm) open at each wrist end and center 20 (22, 24, 26)" [50.8 (55.9, 61, 66)cm] open for the back.

3. Secure the yarn ends, leaving 7" (17.8cm) of C for the wrist ties.

4. Lightly block to the measurements.

5. Optional: Cut fur trim to 18 (20, 22, 24)" [45.7 (50.8, 55.9, 61)cm]. Center and secure it across one back edge.

(See page 47 for details.)

Style Variation

If the fur trim doesn't suit you, don't add it; the shrug has a totally different look without it.

⟨⟨ TIP ⟩⟩

Before you begin your knitting,
be aware that
when you get to the
last three stitches in Row 2
of the Crocus Bud,
you need to do a final "slip."
If you forget this,
you'll have too many stitches
which can ruin
the pattern.

Shrug Diagram

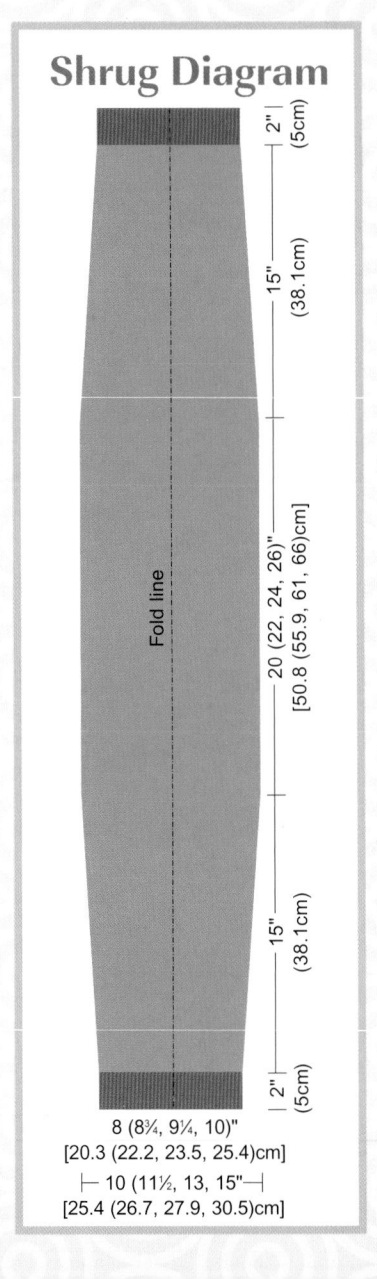

2" (5cm)

15" (38.1cm)

Fold line

20 (22, 24, 26)" [50.8 (55.9, 61, 66)cm]

15" (38.1cm)

2" (5cm)

8 (8¾, 9¼, 10)" [20.3 (22.2, 23.5, 25.4)cm]

⊢ 10 (11½, 13, 15)" ⊣ [25.4 (26.7, 27.9, 30.5)cm]

Adding the Collar and Cuffs

1. To make the cuffs, cut two 8-in. (28.3cm) lengths of faux fur. On each, fold and hem the short sides, using a threaded needle.

2. Fold each rectangle in half lengthwise, wrong sides facing, and use pins to secure. Apply a strip of tape to "tame" the fur. Whipstitch the ribbon edge and the two hemmed sides using a threaded needle. Remove the tape.

3. Cut two 1-in. (2.5cm) lengths of ¾-in.-wide (1.9cm) hook-and-loop tape. Position and sew the loop section to the inside of the ribbon edge, and the hook section to the outside of the ribbon edge as shown.

4. To make the collar, cut a 18-in. (45.7cm) length of faux fur, and follow steps 1–3. Omit the hook-and-loop tape. Center and pin the ribbon edge of the faux fur to the edge of the neckline on the shrug, sewing it in place.

open weave
ponchette

a lacy drape of the silkiest yarn

T his ponchette is perfect for that summer evening when a camisole isn't quite enough but a sweater is too much. The white, open-weave texture is appealing even when it's layered over a plain top. The ponchette can be knitted quickly on size 35 (19mm) needles and sewn together in less than 30 minutes.

SKILL LEVEL
Basic

SIZES
S/M (L/XL)

MEASUREMENTS
- Length: 10 (12)" [25.4 (30.5)cm] after finishing
- Width: 40 (44") [101.6 (111.8)cm]

MATERIALS
- 306 (459) yds. [280 (420)m] fine-weight nylon {two (three) balls Katia "Sevilla" [1¾ oz. (50g)], #03 off-white} (A)
- 285 (380) yds. [261 (348)m] bulky cotton/rayon/nylon blend {three (four) balls Katia "Ola" [1¾ oz. (50g)], #03 off-white} (B)
- Pair US 35 (19mm) needles
- Tapestry needle
- One size K/10.5 (6.5mm) crochet hook for fringe

GAUGE
6 sts and 8 rows to 4" (10cm) measured over St st on US 35 (19mm) needles (or size to obtain gauge).

ABBREVIATIONS
See page 82.

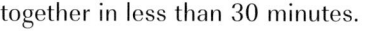

PONCHETTE

Using A and B, cast on 59 (65) sts.

Row 1: WS. K1, *p1, k1; rep from *.

Rows 2-3: *K1, p1; rep from * to the last st, k1.

Rows 4-19 (4-23): Rev st st (k on WS, p on RS).

NECK OPENING

Row 20 (24): RS. P20 (23), BO 19 sts, p to end of row.

Row 21 (25): K20 (23), cast on 19 sts, k to the end of the row.

Rows 22-37 (26-45): Reverse st st.

Rows 38-40 (46-48): Rep rows 1-3. BO k-wise.

FINISHING

1. Fold the ponchette in half length-wise with the neck opening [rows 20-21 (24-25)] at the fold.

2. Using a tapestry needle and both yarns, sew 7-in. (17.8cm) (or desired length) sleeve seams loose-ly to match the gauge of the fabric.

3. Using both yarns, make 5-in. (12.7cm) fringes evenly around the lower edge opening.

Ponchette Pattern

Before sewing

19" (48.3cm)

Fold line

40" x 10" (44" x 12") [101.6 x 25.4 (111.8 x 30.5)cm]

Fold Line

After sewing

TIP

If you haven't used large needles before, take some time practicing with them before you start the project. They'll feel a bit clumsy at first, but because the stitches are loose, precise control of your needles isn't necessary.

Style Variation

Because the featured yarn has a glossy finish, the ponchette has an elegant luster that makes it a perfect piece to go with an evening dress. Make it in jet black yarn for a different look.

faux fur
capelet
or muffler

*light-as-a-
feather
luxury*

Little compares to the romance of a classic little cape knitted up in a faux fur yarn. The feel of the garment is sublimeley soft, and the lightweight character of the garment makes it very comfortable to wear. The combination of violet and black yarns produces a texture that shimmers with variegated color. The

SKILL LEVEL
Basic

MEASUREMENTS
- Length: 6¼" (15.9cm)
- Width: 16" (40.6cm) at neck edge; 34" (86.4cm) at lower edge

MATERIALS
- 180 yds. (162m) each, 2 colors bulky polyester faux fur {three balls each Lion Brand "Fun Fur" [1¾ oz. (50g)], #191 violet (A) and #153 black (B)}
- Pair US 11 (8mm) needles
- Stitch markers
- Tapestry needle
- Closure: Brooch or ribbon ties [1.5" x 48" (3.8 x 121.9cm)]— satin or velvet ribbon, sewing needle, and matching thread

GAUGE
16 sts and 32 rows to 4" (10cm) measured over garter st with 1 strand A and B held tog on US 11(8mm) needles (or size to obtain gauge).

ABBREVIATIONS
See page 82.

appeal of faux fur yarn is that it doesn't take itself seriously. It clearly has the look of fur but in fun colors not found in nature. For a more formal look, work up the capelet in jet black yarns, adding a brilliant, high voltage rhinestone brooch at the neck for dazzling contrast. For a more sophisticated look, perhaps one for daytime wear, knit up the capelet in earthier tones like chocolate and cinnamon, pairing it with a tweed jacket. In general, the closer in shade the color of the yarns, the softer and more restrained the colors will appear. So versatile, this capelet might become a favorite piece in your wardrobe.

CAPELET

With one strand each A and B held tog, cast on 136 sts.
Row 1 (RS): [K19, pm] 6 times.
Row 2: [K to 2 sts before marker, k2tog, sm] 3 times; k19; [sm, ssk, k to marker] 2 times, sm, k2tog, k to end. [130 sts]
Rows 3–5: K.
Rows 6–49: Rep [Rows 2-5] 11 times. [64 sts]
BO all the sts.

FINISHING
Brooch: Pin the neck opening closed.

Ribbon ties: Cut a 48-in. (121.9cm) length of ribbon in half. Sew one end of each length to either side of the neck opening.

Style Variation

You will be inspired to wear your capelet in a variety of ways, depending on the occasion and your mood. Instead of arranging it on your shoulders as shown, wrap the capelet around your neck, muffler style, and overlap the sides.

⟨TIP⟩

Expressing your personal style is easy. For a glamorous look, close the capelet with an oversized rhinestone brooch. Choose one with stones in a similar colorway for a subtle glint of sparkle, or wear an over-the-top piece of jewelry, like a pin with quartz crystals in complementary colors—such as chartreuse or orange—that gently clash with the capelet.

ballet-style
sweater

a modern take

on a classic

This sweater is for the woman who loves ballet tradition— the side-to-side design even mimics dance movement. The knitting flows easily with little finish work, producing a great sweater in very little time. The fashionable cropped, double-wrapped sweater is trimmed in "fur" that further defines the graceful lines of the bodice, waist, and cuffs.

SKILL LEVEL Intermediate

MEASUREMENTS
- Length: 13 (14, 15, 16)" [33 (35.6, 38.1, 40.6)cm]
- Back width: 17 (19, 21, 23)" [43.2 (48.3, 53.3, 58.4)cm]

MATERIALS
- 588 (672, 756, 840) yds. [539 (616, 693, 770)m] cashmere or cashmere blend {seven (eight, nine, ten) balls Lion brand "Lion Cashmere Blend" [1¼ oz. (40g)], #101 light pink} (A)
- 137 yds. (125m) lightweight fuzzy nylon {one ball Lion Brand "Tiffany: Article 260" [1¾ oz. (50g)], #101 light pink} (B)
- 399 yds. (365m) medium-weight rayon/nylon blend {one ball South West Trading Company "Melody" [3½ oz. (100g)], #115 fuchsia} (C)
- 81 yds. (75m) superbulky nylon/cotton/acrylic blend {one ball Tahki "Poppy" [1.8 oz. (50g)], #10 pink} (D)
- 17 yds. (15.5m) superbulky acrylic boa yarn {one hank Plymouth "Foxy" [1¼ oz. (40g)], #25 pink} (E)
- One US 8 (5mm) 24" (60cm) circular needle, pair US 36 (20mm) needles
- Stitch holders
- Tapestry needle

GAUGE
16 sts and 24 rows to 4" (10cm) measured over st st with A on US 8 (5mm) needles (or size to obtain gauge).

ABBREVIATIONS
See page 82.

SWEATER

RIGHT SIDE

Sleeve

Starting at bottom of the sleeve, with one strand each A and B held tog using US 8 (5mm) circular needle, cast on 31 (33, 35, 37) sts.

Rows 1-11: Beg with a p row, stockinette st (k on RS, p on WS). Drop B.

Rows 12-17: With A only, st st.

Row 18 (RS): K2, m1, k to the last 2 sts, m1, k2. [33 (35, 37, 39) sts]

Rows 19-23: St st.

Rows 24-71 (71, 77, 77): Rep rows 18-23. [49 (51, 55, 57) sts after row 71 (71, 77, 77)]

Work even in st st until the sleeve measures 17 (17, 17½, 17½) in. [43.2 (43.2, 44.5, 44.5)cm] or a desired length.

Do not cut the yarn.

Back

Cast on 28 (31, 33, 36) sts at the beg of the next 2 rows. [105 (113, 121, 129) sts] Work even in st st for 4.5 (5.5, 6.5, 7.5) in. [11.4 (14, 16.5, 19)cm, ending after a WS row.

Row 1 (RS): K53 (56, 60, 64) and place these sts on a holder for the

front. K to the end of the row. [54 (57, 61, 65) sts]

Row 2: P.

Row 3: K1, ssk, k to the end of the row.

Rows 4-5: Rep rows 2-3. [51 (54, 58, 62) sts]

Rows 6-26: St st.
BO loosely.

Front

Transfer 54 (57, 61, 65) front sts from the first holder to US 8 (5mm) circular needle. With WS facing, join A and B at the neck edge.

Row 1: WS. BO 12 (13, 14, 15) sts; drop B (but do not cut) and p with A to the end of the row. [42 (44, 47, 50) sts]

Row 2: K to the last 4 sts; with A and B, ssk, k2tog; drop B.

Row 3: With A, p.

Rows 4-9: Rep rows 2-3. [34 (36, 39, 42) sts after row 9]

Row 10: K to the last 2 sts; with A and B, k2tog.; drop B.

Row 11: With A, p.

Rows 12-55 (59, 65, 71): Rep rows 10-11. [11 sts after row 55 (59, 65, 71)]
BO loosely.

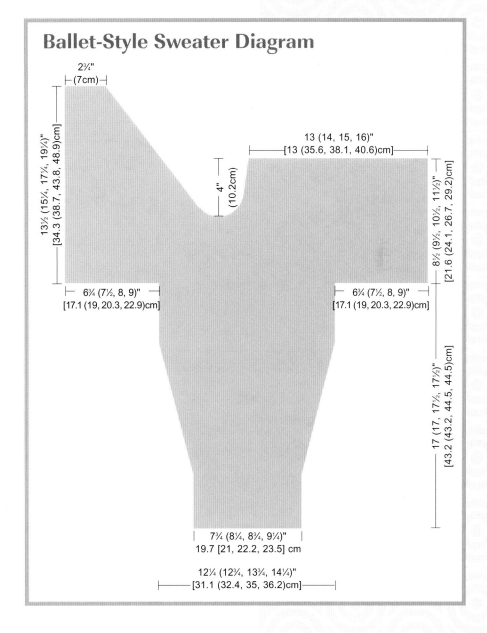

Ballet-Style Sweater Diagram

2¾"
[7cm]

13½ (15¼, 17¼, 19¼)"
[34.3 (38.7, 43.8, 48.9)cm]

4"
(10.2cm)

13 (14, 15, 16)"
[13 (35.6, 38.1, 40.6)cm]

8½ (9½, 10½, 11½)"
[21.6 (24.1, 26.7, 29.2)cm]

6¾ (7½, 8, 9)"
[17.1 (19, 20.3, 22.9)cm]

6¾ (7½, 8, 9)"
[17.1 (19, 20.3, 22.9)cm]

17 (17, 17½, 17½)"
[43.2 (43.2, 44.5, 44.5)cm]

7¾ (8¼, 8¾, 9¼)"
19.7 [21, 22.2, 23.5] cm

12¼ (12¾, 13¾, 14¼)"
[31.1 (32.4, 35, 36.2)cm]

LEFT SIDE

Sleeve

Work same as for right side.

Back

Cast on 28 (31, 33, 36) sts at beg of the next 2 rows. [105 (113, 121, 129) sts] Work even in St st for 4½ (5½, 6½, 7½) in. [11.4 (14, 16.5, 19)cm], ending after a WS row.

Row 1 (RS): K54 (57, 61, 65). Place the rem 53 (56, 60, 64) sts on a holder for the front.

Row 2: P.

Row 3: K to the last 3 sts, k2tog, k1.

Rows 4-5: Rep rows 2–3. [51 (54, 58, 62) sts]

Rows 6-26: St st.

BO loosely.

Front

Transfer 54 (57, 61, 65) sts from the stitch holder to a US 8 (5mm) circular needle. With RS facing, join A and B at neck edge.

Row 1: RS. BO 12 (13, 14, 15) sts; drop B (but do not cut) and k with A to the end of the row. [42 (44, 47, 50) sts]

Row 2: P.

Row 3: With A and B, ssk, k2tog; drop B, k to the end of the row.

Rows 4-9: Rep rows 2-3. [34 (36, 39, 42) sts after row 9]

Row 10: With A, p.

Row 11: With A and B, ssk; drop B, k to the end of the row.

Rows 12-55 (59, 65, 71): Rep rows 10-11. [11 sts after row 55 (59, 65, 71)]

BO loosely.

TIP

Lightly baste the trim so it is easily removed; you may decide later to use different trim or none at all.

BOA EDGING AND SASH

With A, B and C held tog on US 36 (20mm) needles, loosely cast on 136 (140, 144, 148) sts.

Row 1: K.

Row 2: *K1, m1; rep from * to end.

Row 3: K.

BO loosely.

FINISHING

1. Sew the sleeve and side seams, leaving a 2 in. (5cm) opening at the right side seam ¼ in. (0.64cm) from the lower edge.

2. Sew the back seam to join the right and left sides.

3. Block the sweater to your measurements.

4. Fold the boa edging in half, and pin the fold to back neck seam. With a tapestry needle and B, secure it along neck and front opening.

5. Cut C and D into various lengths and attach randomly to boa.

6. Attach three various-length strands to each sleeve cuff.

POM-POMS

(optional)

With A, B, and C held together and using US 36 (20mm) needles, pick up 3 sts at the end of the tie.

Row 1: K1, *m1, k1; rep from * to the end of the row.

Rep row 1 five times more. BO leaving a long tail. Thread a tapestry needle with the tail; roll the fabric into a ball, and sew it into a pom-pom shape.

There are many ways to approach circular knitting. For more details consult "Sources & Resources."

cummerbund
belt

with

tassel ties

A versatile accessory, the cummerbund has long extensions meant to cross in the back and tie in the front. The ribbon yarns, beads, and tassels embellish the wool-like garment, making it perfect for dressy occasions but not too dressy to wear with casual slacks—or even jeans.

SKILL LEVEL Basic

SIZES
S-M (L-XL)

MEASUREMENTS
- Front: 5¼ x 15¼ (17¾)" [13.25 x 38.5 (45cm)], excluding ties
- Ties: 32 in. (81.25cm) each

MATERIALS
- 197 yds. (180m) medium-weight acrylic/wool blend {one ball Lion Brand "Wool-Ease Worsted" [3 oz. (85g)], #123 seaspray} (A)
- 109 yds. (100m) [218 yds. (200m)] lightweight nylon {one (two) balls Anny Blatt "Victoria" [1¾ oz. (50g)], #156 Celeste} (B)
- 153 yds. (140m) fine-weight nylon {one ball Katia "Sevilla" [1¾ oz. (50g)], #56 lime green} (C)
- Pair each US 7 (4.5mm) needles, US 9 (5.5mm) needles
- Sewing needle and thread to match A
- 4 buttons with shanks
- 8 round beads, 7mm

GAUGE
13 sts and 24 rows to 4" (10cm) measured over basketweave st on US 7 (4.5mm) needles (or size to obtain gauge).

ABBREVIATIONS
See page 82.

CUMMERBUND

FRONT

With US 7 (4.5mm) needles and A, B, and C held tog, cast on 50 (58) sts.

Rows 1 and 3: *K1, p1; rep from * to the last st.

Row 2: *P1, k1; rep from * to the last st. Change to US 9 (5.5mm) needles.

Rows 4-6: Rep rows 2, 1 and 2.

Rows 7 and 9 (RS): K1, [p1, k1] twice, [k4, p4] 5 (6) times, [p1, k1] twice, p1.

Rows 8 and 10: P1, [k1, p1] twice, [k4, p4] 5 (6) times, [k1, p1] twice, k1.

Rows 11 and 13: K1, [p1, k1] twice, [p4, k4] 5 (6) times, [p1, k1] twice, p1.

Rows 12 and 14: P1, [k1, p1] twice, [p4, k4] 5 (6) times, [k1, p1] twice, k1.

Rows 15-22: Rep rows 7-14.

Rows 23-26: Rep rows 7-10.

Rows 27-29: Rep rows 1-3. Change to US 7 (4.5mm) needles.

Rows 30-31: Rep rows 2 and 1. BO foll row 2 of the patt.

TIE

With RS facing and A and B held tog, use US 7 (4.5mm) needles to pick up 19 sts along the side edge of the front.

Row 1 (WS): [K1, p1] acrs row.

Row 2: K.

Row 3: P.

Row 4 (dec): K2, k2tog, k to last 4 sts, k2tog, k2.

Rows 5-10: Repeat rows 1-2. [11 sts]

Rows 11-31: Work in st st. Change to US 9 (5.5mm) needles.

Row 32: Rep row 3. [9 sts]

Rows 33-51: Work in st st.

Row 52: Rep row 3. [7 sts]

Rows 53-71: Work in st st.

Row 72: K1, k2tog, k to last 3 sts, k2tog, k1. [5 sts]

Rows 73-91: Work in st st.

Row 92: K1, k2tog, k2. [4 sts]

Rows 93-99: Work in st st.

Row 100: K1, k2tog, k1. [3 sts]

Rows 100-150: Work in st st. BO. Rep on the other side.

TASSELS

Make two 3-in. (7.6cm) tassels with C. Embellish the top of each tassel by sewing on two buttons (on the front and the back) and four beads (opposite sides between the buttons). Of course, you can embellish the tassels any way you like.

TO FINISH

If desired, sew the edges of the ties to form tubes, beg 5 in. (12.7cm) from the front to the end. Attach tassels to the ends of the ties.

TIP

It's a good idea to run a threaded sewing needle through the center of the tassel several times to secure the slippery yarns, which have a natural tendency to slide.

Wax your beading thread to reduce tangling and to strengthen the thread.

Style Variation

The cummerbund instantly transforms the look of a plain pair of dress trousers.

felted
belt

with beaded trim

T his eye-catching belt is the perfect accessory. It looks elegant paired with a classic black dinner jacket. With jeans and a white shirt, it accentuates the strong color contrasts among the pieces. The belt is worked in simple garter stitch. Then the fabric is laundered in a felting (or fulling) process that tightens the texture, creating a smooth, sturdy foundation for the beaded lace trim.

SKILL LEVEL
Basic

SIZES
S/M/L

MEASUREMENTS
(Post-felting)
- Length: Approx. 33/36/39" (83.8/91.4/99cm)
- Width: Approx. 6¼" (16.9cm)

MATERIALS
- 158 yds. (144m) medium-weight wool {one ball Lion Brand "Lion Wool" [3 oz. (85g)], #153 black}
- Pair US 9 (5.5mm) needles
- Beaded trim, 4 x 36/39/42" (10.2 x 91.4/99/106.7cm)
- Narrow beaded trim, 1½" x 18" (3.8cm x 45.7cm)
- Three pairs covered hooks and eyes, ¾" (1.9cm)
- Sewing needle and matching thread
- Tapestry needle
- Straight pins
- For felting: washing machine, measuring tape, mesh bag, detergent, lint-free towel.

GAUGE
16 sts and 8 rows to 4" (10cm) measured over garter st on US 9 (5.5mm) needles pre-felting (or size to obtain gauge).

ABBREVIATIONS
See page 82.

BELT

Cast on 35 sts. K every row until the belt measures 38/42/45 in. (96.5 /106.7/114.3cm) long. BO K-wise.

FELTING

Shrinking wool so that it appears felted is not an exact art. The triple action of soap, water, and agitation causes knitted wool to shrink at a rate that is difficult to control. However, the felting process creates an appealing texture that is flat and sturdy, making otherwise easy-to-see stitches disappear. This effect can serve the beginner knitter who may have to cover up a few mistakes, which are typically part of the learning process.

1. Insert the belt into a mesh bag or pillowcase that you can close securely. Place the bag in the washing machine with detergent, and run the hot wash and cold rinse cycles. To increase friction, a necessary part of the process, add lint-free items to the tub. (A pair of faded jeans works well.) Check the belt often to make sure it doesn't get too small!

2. When the cycle is finished or the knitted fabric is the desired size, remove it and lay it flat on a towel. If necessary, repeat Step 1 until the fabric is reduced to the desired size.

3. Block the wet fabric on the towel, flattening and stretching the piece into an evenly shaped band measuring 33/36/39 x 6.25 in. (83.8/ 91.4/99 x 15.9cm). Let it dry completely.

DECORATING

1. Lay the belt horizontally on a flat work surface.

2. Center and pin the length of wide beaded trim to the belt, folding under the raw edges at the ends and pinning to secure them.

3. Thread a sewing needle with matching thread, and sew the trim to the belt, using short running stitches as follows: begin at one short end, and continue along one long side, adjusting the trim as necessary; go back to the short side, and sew along the remaining long side, keeping the trim flat; sew the second short side to the belt; then, use tiny stitches to tack the central section of the trim to the belt.

Remove the pins.

4. To finish, measure and cut two equal lengths of the narrow trim to the width of the belt plus 1 in. (2.5cm)

5. Lay one length of trim flush with the outside edge of the belt, folding under the raw edges at the top and bottom to the wrong side of the fabric.

6. Secure the trim using short, neat running stitches.

7. Repeat steps 5-6 to secure the second length of trim to the opposite end of the belt.

CLOSURES

Position and sew hooks and eyes on the WS of the belt, following the diagram, below, or as desired.

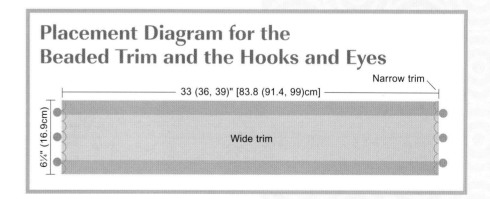

Placement Diagram for the Beaded Trim and the Hooks and Eyes

Narrow trim

33 (36, 39)" [83.8 (91.4, 99)cm]

6¼" (16.9cm)

Wide trim

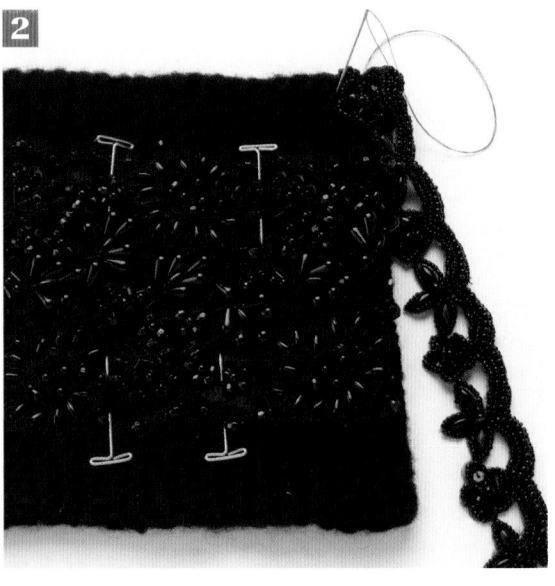

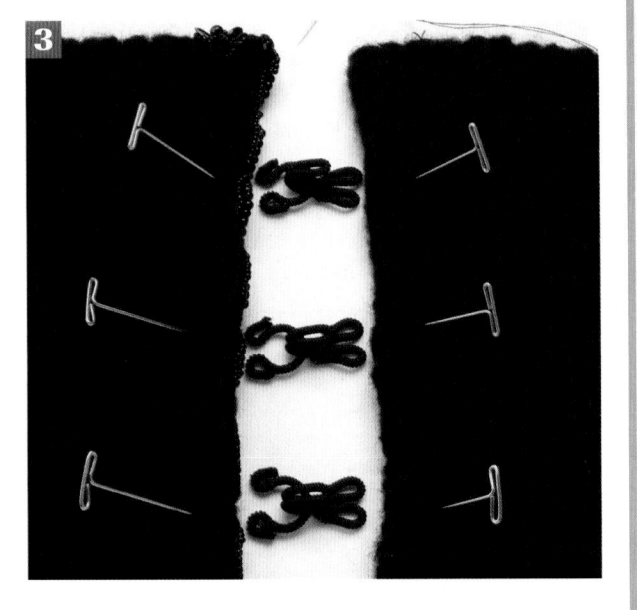

The Secrets to Adding the Beaded Trim

1. Center and pin the wide trim to the belt, folding under the trim at the short sides. Secure the layers by running the pins vertically to accommodate the natural stretch of the knitted fabric. Make certain the folds are neat and even with the knitted edge. If any beads come loose while you are working, save them so that you can fill in any bare areas on the trim after it is secured. Sew the trim to the belt using a double-strand of matching thread without tugging too vigorously on the thread so that the band of trim remains flat. Try "hiding" your stitches between the beaded detail for a professional-looking finish.

2. Center and pin one length of narrow trim to one short side of belt, folding the raw edges at the top and bottom to the wrong side of the knitted fabric. (If necessary, reinforce some of the beads, using a threaded needle or beading glue.) Be aware that the added layer of trim will add some bulk to the short edges of the belt. This extra thickness will add to the structure of the belt. Sew the trim in place, "hiding" your stitches between the beads, and tacking the edge of the trim to the beaded trim applied in step 1. Repeat to add trim to the other edge of the belt.

3. Position and sew 3 sets of hooks and eyes to the edges of the belt. Note that the hook-and-eye style used here is the silk-wrapped kind where the metal findings are concealed with windings of thick thread that blend nicely with the knitted fabric. To sew the pairs on, begin by turning the belt to the wrong side. Adjust the edges so that they line up as closely as possible. (Felted knit fabric has a tendency to produce slightly unequal shrinking so the edges may not be exactly equal in measurement.) Use T-pins to mark the positions of each pair. Then sew on one pair at a time.

The felted belt is a signature piece whether it is worn over a formal jacket or with jeans and a tailored oxford shirt. The appeal of the belt is its strong character. It is extra wide and bold, mixing a casual knitted fabric with an "over-the-top" band of beads and lace. Soft to the touch but sturdy enough to stand up at the waist without "collapsing" in unattractive folds, the felted knit fabric gives the belt the needed structure without constricting the waist due to the slight "give" intrinsic to all knitted fabrics. To add more style to your look when wearing the belt, pair it with other signature accessories like a cowboy hat and boots, or whatever items in your wardrobe make this accessory your own.

Variation

Instead of applying a wide band of beaded trim in black or a color that matches your belt, consider using embroidered appliqués instead. Here, scrollwork and floral motifs are arranged in a lovely border design at the top and bottom edges of the knitted band. For a peasant look, choose heart, flower, and leaf appliqués.

vintage
pink
belt

spring's soft shades

T his ultra-feminine wool belt worked in seed stitch has an iridescent belt buckle reminiscent of '40s style. Knitted on small needles, the band is made using a double strand of extra-fine yarn in the softest pastel that produces a firm and reversible belt fabric that won't curl.

SKILL LEVEL
Basic

MEASUREMENTS
- Length: 31½" (80cm)
- Width: 2½" (6.4cm), excluding buckle tab. (Adjust measurements to fit wearer.)

MATERIALS
- 137 yds. (125m) lightweight wool {one ball Filatura di Crosa "Zara" [1¾ oz. (50g)], #1510 pink}
- Pair US 2 (2.75mm) needles
- One round plastic buckle (2.75 x 2.25" [7 x 5.7cm]) in pearlescent aqua (M&J Trimmings)
- Tapestry needle

GAUGE
20 sts and 29 rows to 4" (10cm) measured over seed st on US 2 (2.75mm) needles (or size to obtain gauge).

ABBREVIATIONS
See page 82.

The seed stitch is simple to remember: stitches that are knit on one row are purled on the next row, and stitches that are purled on one row are knit on the following row. By alternating the knit and purl stitches, a fabric with delicate and visible texture appears. When the band is paired with the glowing patina of the buckle, a belt of classic elegance is created.

BELT

With 2 strands A held tog (one end from inside of ball and one end from outside), cast on 12 sts.
Row 1: RS. *K1, p1; rep from * to the end.
Row 2: *P1, k1; rep from * to the end.
Rep rows 1-2 for seed stitch until the piece measures 31 in. (78.7cm) long or the desired length.

TAB

Row 1: RS. K2tog, *k1, p1; rep from * to the end.
Row 2: K2tog, *p1, k1; rep from * to the last st, p1.
Row 3: K2tog, *p1, k1; rep from * to the end.
Row 4: K2tog, *k1, p1; rep from * to the last st, k1.
Row 5: K2tog, *k1, p1; rep from * to the end. [7 sts]
Row 6: *P1, k1; rep from * to the last st, p1.
Rep row 6 for 1½ in. (3.8cm).
BO, leaving a 6-in. (15.2cm) tail.

FINISHING

1. With the WS of buckle facing you, thread the tab around the center post of the buckle and back to the WS.
2. Fold over the tab, and secure it using a tapestry needle and the tail of yarn.

HELPFUL HINTS
Fitting:
The fit of the belt is a simple matter of measuring the waist and adding several inches to accommodate the belt flap that extends beyond the buckle. Reduce the length of the flap, if desired, or increase it to form a piece that is long enough to wrap around the belt.

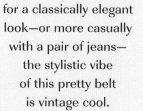

TIP
Perfect to wear around the waist of a pretty skirt or dress for a classically elegant look—or more casually with a pair of jeans—the stylistic vibe of this pretty belt is vintage cool.

Style Variation
One of the key elements of belt style is the buckle. Here, a "patent" rectangle updates the look of the vintage belt.

cabled
armlets

*feminine
and funky*

M ade of super-soft baby-blue yarn, these armlets look darling peeking out of coat or jacket sleeves, while providing that extra bit of warmth needed on frigid days. They can easily be worn under or over long-sleeved sweaters or as a stylish complement to a short-sleeved sweater. They also look great with a dainty embroidered blouse or dress.

SKILL LEVEL
Intermediate

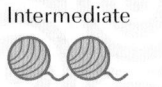

SIZES
S/M (L/XL)

MEASUREMENTS
■ Length: 12½" (31.8cm) without ruffle
■ Wrist circumference: 6 (7½)" [15.2 (19)cm]
■ Arm circumference: 9 (10½)" [22.9 (26.7)cm]
■ Ruffle: 2" (5cm)

MATERIALS
■ 252 yds. (231m) medium-weight cashmere or cashmere blend (three balls Lion Brand "Lion Cashmere Blend," #105 light blue)
■ Pair each US 9 (5.5mm) needles, US 7 (4.5mm) needles
■ Cable needle
■ Tapestry needle

GAUGE
24 sts and 26 rows to 4" (10cm) measured over k1, p1 rib on US 7 (4.5mm) needles (or size to obtain gauge).

ABBREVIATIONS
See page 82.

SPECIAL STITCHES

Knit in Front and Back (kfb): Knit into the front and the back of next stitch.

Increase 1 st (inc1): Knit into the stitch in the row below. This creates an almost invisible increase and can be worked from the right or left (as in this pattern) of the stitch.

Cable 4 Back (C4B) (uses 4 consecutive sts): Slip 2 stitches onto CN and hold them in back; knit 2 stitches from the LN; then knit 2 stitches from the CN.

ARMLET (MAKE 2)

With US 7 (4.5mm) needles and A, cast on 34 (42) sts.

Row 1: RS. K1, *[p1, k1] 2 (4) times, p1, k4; rep from* to last 6 sts; end [p1, k1] 3 (5) times.

Row 2: P1, *[k1, p1] 2 (4) times, k1, p4; rep from* to the last 6 sts; end [k1, p1] 3 (5) times.

Row 3: K1, *[p1, k1] 2 (4) times, p1, C4B; rep from* to the last 6 sts; end [p1, k1] 3 (5) times.

Row 4: Rep row 2.

Rows 5-28: Rep [Rows 1-4] 6 times.

Row 29 (inc): [K1, p1] 2 (4) times, kfb AND inc1 all in next st, p1, *k4, [p1, k1] twice, p1; rep from * to the

last 10 sts, k4, p1, kfb AND inc1 all in next st, [p1, k1] 2 (4) times. [38 (46) sts, 8 (12) sts in each border rib]

Rows 30-46: Cont in the pattern as established, incorporating 4 additional border sts.

Row 47 (inc): [K1, p] 2 (4) times, kfb AND inc1 all in the next st, p1, k1, p1, *k4, [p1, k1] twice, p1; rep from * to the last 12 sts, k4, p1, k1, p1, kfb/inc1 in next st, [p1, k1] 2 (4) times. [42 (50) sts, 10 (14) sts in each border rib]

Rows 48-64: Cont in the patt as established, incorporating 4 additional border sts.

Row 65 (inc): [K1, p1] 2 (4) times, kfb AND inc1 all in the next st, [p1, k1] twice, p1, *k4, [p1, k1] twice, p1; rep from * to the last 14 sts, k4, [p1, k1] twice, p1, kfb AND inc1 all in the next st, [p1, k1] 2 (4) times. [46 (54) sts, 12 (16) sts in each border rib]

Rows 66-76: Cont in the patt as established, incorporating 4 additional border sts.

Row 77: K1, [p1, k1] 8 (10) times, m1, p1, [k1, p1] 3 times, k2tog, [p1, k1] 10 (12) times.

Row 78: *P1, k1; rep from * to last st, p1.

Row 79: *K1, p1; rep from * to the last st, k1.

BO foll row 78.

RUFFLE

With RS facing, pick up 34 (42) stitches along the wrist edge. Change to US 7 (4.5mm) needle if picking up sts with the smaller needle.

Row 1 (WS): P.

Row 2: K.

Row 3: P.

Row 4 (inc): *Kfb; rep from * to end. [68 (84) sts]

Change to US 9 (5.5mm) needles.

Row 5: P.

Row 6: K.

Row 7: P.

Row 8 (inc): *Kfb; rep from * to the end. [136 (168) sts]

Row 9: P.

Row 10: K.

BO p-wise.

FINISHING

Block the armlets to your measurements. With A and RS facing, sew the seams through the centers of the edge sts.

NOTE: *If you enjoyed knitting cables in the Extra-Chunky Ponchette, you'll be glad to have another opportunity to work with them. This time, instead of making chunky cables with correspondingly large knitting and cable needles, you will use thinner knitting and cable needles to produce more delicate cables.*

TIP

Once you've completed the first four rows— with the exception of the cables on row 3— all you need to do is "knit the knits and purl the purls."

Reset row counter after every four-row set, and record each set as it is completed.

It's easier to pick up stitches with a needle that is smaller than the one used to knit the piece.

fingerless
gloves

*combining style
and substance*

These fingerless gloves—or gauntlets—have it all: form and function. They start with a traditional lace pattern; then the hand is knitted fingerless, a modern touch; and finally, they are embellished with gorgeous buttons. An added bonus is that they'll keep your arms and hands toasty. Enjoy wearing these unique gloves, and accept the compliments.

SKILL LEVEL
Intermediate

MEASUREMENTS
■ Length: 15" (38.1cm)
■ Wrist circumference: 8" (20.3cm)
■ Arm circumference: 15" (38.1cm) buttoned

MATERIALS
■ 198 yds. (180m) fine-weight mohair/acrylic blend {one ball Filatura di Crosa "Multicolor" [1¾ oz. (50g)], #3053 garnet} (A)
■ 162 yds. (150m) lightweight merino wool/cashmere blend {two balls Kertzer "Truffles" [⅞ oz. (25g)], #2144 garnet} (B)
■ Pair US 6 (4mm) needles
■ Set of five US 5 (3.75mm) double-pointed needles
■ Tapestry needle
■ Ten ⅝" (16mm) round buttons

GAUGE
24 sts and 28 rows to 4" (10cm) measured over k3, p2 rib on US 6 (4mm) needles (or size to obtain gauge).

ABBREVIATIONS
See page 82.

GLOVES

RIGHT GLOVE

With US 6 (4mm) needles and one strand each A and B held tog, cast on 50 sts.

Row 1: WS. [P15, pm] 3 times, *[k1, p1] twice, k1*.

Row 2: *[K1, p1] twice, k1*, [k1, yo, k3, ssk, yo, sk2p, yo, k2tog, k3, yo, k1] 3 times.

Row 3: K to the last marker, *[k1, p1] twice, k1*.

Row 4: *[K1, p1] twice*, k1, p to the end of the row.

Rows 5-8: Rep rows 1-4.

Row 9 (buttonhole): P to the last marker, *k1, bind off the next 2 sts, k1*.

Row 10: *K1, p1, cast on 2 sts, k1*, [k1, yo, k3, ssk, yo, sk2p, yo, k2tog, k3, yo, k1] 3 times.

Rows 11-12: Rep rows 3-4.

Row 13: P to the last marker, *[k1, p1] twice, k1*.

Row 14: *[K1, p1] twice, k1*, [k1, yo, k3, ssk, yo, sk2p, yo, k2tog, k3, yo, k1] 3 times.

Row 15-16: Rep rows 13-14.

Row 17: K to the last marker, *[k1, p1] twice, k1*.

Row 18: Rep row 14.

Rows 19-20 (buttonhole): Rep rows 9-10.

Row 21: K to the last marker, *[k1, p1] twice, k1*.

Row 22: *[K1, p1] twice, k1*, [k1, yo, k3, ssk, yo, sk2p, yo, k2tog, k3, yo, k1] 3 times.

Row 23: P to the last marker, *[k1, p1] twice, k1*.

Rows 24-30: Rep rows 22-23.

Rows 31-32 (buttonhole): Rep rows 9-10.

Row 33: K to the last marker, *[k1, p1] twice, k1*.

Row 34: *[K1, p1] twice, k1*, p to the end of the row.

Row 35: P to the last marker; *[k1, p1] twice, k1*.

Row 36: *[K1, p1] twice, k1*, [k1, yo, k2, ssk, yo, sk2p, yo, k2tog, k2, yo, k1] 3 times.

Rows 37-42: Rep rows 35-36.

Rows 43-44 (buttonhole): Rep rows 9-10.

Rows 45-54: Rep rows 35-36.

Rows 55-56 (buttonhole): Rep rows 9-10.

Row 57: K to the last marker, *[k1, p1] twice, k1*.

Change to dpns.

Hand

Rnd 1: BO 5 sts, p to the end of the rnd. [45 sts]

Rnd 2: P.

Rnd 3: *K3, p2; rep from * to end of rnd.

Rep rnd 3 for 2½ in. (6.35cm) or a desired length to the base of the thumb.

Thumb opening

Next rnd: Rib 25 sts, bind off the next 8 sts, rib to the end of the rnd.

Next rnd: Rib 25 sts, cast on 8 sts, rib to the end of the rnd.

Continue to rep rnd 3 for 2 in. (5cm) or a desired length.

BO firmly in the patt.

Thumb

With dpns and A and B held tog, pick up 8 sts across the bound-off sts, 1 st in the corner, 8 sts across the cast-on sts, 1 st in the corner, pm.

Dec rnd: [K7, ssk] twice. [16 sts]

Work even in st st (k every rnd) for 1¾ in. (4.45cm) or to the desired length.

BO k-wise.

LEFT GLOVE

Work the same as the right glove with the following exceptions:

If the stitches between * * (buttonhole band) fall at the end of the row, work them at the beg of the row.

If stitches between * * (buttonhole band) fall at the beg of row, work *(continued at top of next column)*

them at the end of row.

Row 58: P.

Work Row 59: BO 5 sts, k to the end of the row. [45 sts]

Change to dpns.

Hand

Rnd 1: *P2, k3; rep from * to the end of the rnd.

Rep rnd 1 for 2½ in. (6.35cm) or desired length to base of thumb.

Thumb opening

Next rnd: Rib 17, BO next 8 sts, rib to the end of rnd.

Next rnd: Rib 17, cast on 8 sts, rib to the end of rnd.

Finish the remainder of the left glove same as for right glove.

FINISHING

1. Overlap the bound-off buttonhole-band sts, and stitch them in place.

2. Sew the buttons opposite the buttonholes.

TIP

Try using two 8-in. (20.3cm) plastic circular needles instead of US 5 (3.75mm) double-pointed needles.

chunky
purse
with wooden handles

This superbulky 100 percent wool yarn is a delight to work with. As you knit, you will enjoy its ultra-soft hand and the rich saturated colors of the strand as they change from one deep pastel to the next. The fuzzy white wool used for the border, turquoise buttons, and wooden handles complete the list of natural materials used in the project. Fun to make, the bag is even more fun to wear.

SKILL LEVEL
Basic

MEASUREMENTS
◼ Height: 7½" (21.6cm) without handle
◼ Width: 11½" (29.2cm)

MATERIALS
◼ 54.7 yds. (50m) superbulky wool {one ball Colinette Yarns "Point 5" [3 ½ oz. (100g)], #89 white multi} (A)
◼ 80 yds. (74m) bulky wool {one ball Bouton d'Or "Norma" [1¾ oz. (50g)], #050 white} (B)
◼ Pair each US 7 (4.5mm) needles, US 13 (9mm) needles
◼ Set of wooden purse handles: 4" x 6" (10.2 x 16.5cm)
◼ Tapestry needle
◼ 10 buttons

GAUGE
9.5 sts and 13 rows to 4" (10cm) measured over St st on US 24 (9mm) needles (or size to obtain gauge).

ABBREVIATIONS
See page 82.

PURSE

With US 13 (9mm) needles and A, cast on 17 sts.

Row 1 (RS): K.

Row 2: P.

Row 3 (inc): K5, m1, k to the last 5 sts, m1, k5. [19 sts]

Rows 4-6: St st (k on RS, p on WS).

Rows 7-22: Rep [Rows 3-6] 4 times. [27 sts after row 22]

Row 23: Rep row 3. [29 sts]

Row 24: P.

Row 25 (dec): K5, k2tog; k to the last 6 sts; k2tog, k4. [27 sts]

Rows 26-28: St st.

Rows 29-44: Rep [Rows 25-28] 4 times. [19 sts after row 44]

Row 45: K5, k2tog; k to the last 6 sts; k2tog, k4. [17 sts]

Row 46: P.

Row 47: K.

BO p-wise.

BORDER (Make 2)

With US 7 (4.5mm) needles and B, cast on 32 sts, leaving a long tail for finishing.

Rows 1-8: St st.

Rows 9 and 10: *K1, p1; rep from * to the end.

Rows 11 and 12: *P1, k1; rep from * to the end.

Rows 13-16: Rep rows 9-12. BO foll row 9, leaving a long tail for finishing.

FINISHING

1. Block the pieces to measurements. Fold the purse in half lengthwise with WS tog so that cast-on and bound-off edges are tog. Use A to sew the side seams, leaving the top open 1 in. (2.5cm).

2. Fold the border in half lengthwise with WS tog. Insert the base of the handle, center, and tack it securely in place. Thread the tail in the tapestry needle, and sew the top and side seams closed, working tightly around the handles. Repeat for the other handle.

3. With RS facing, position the border to overlap the top 1-in. (2.5cm) edge and, using B, sew it in place. Repeat on the other side.

4. Attach five evenly spaced buttons to each side of border. If desired, make a fabric lining, and sew it to the inside of the purse.

KNITTING BASICS

getting started

You're inspired! You've seen a great-looking scarf or a cool poncho, each knitted in a fabulous yarn, and you're all set to begin knitting. Whether you're a beginner or veteran knitter, check out the information in this section to ensure a fun and productive knitting experience.

all you need to know to knit like a pro

basic tools

A s with any craft, knitting is facilitated by tools that make all the difference between struggling or sailing through the process, as well as enabling quality results. Some essential tools are:

1. Scissors (curved scissors are great for shaping pom-poms)
2. Hem guage and ruler
3. Darning needles (blunt ends, large eyes; come in various sizes).
4. Locking stitch markers (look like big safety pins)
5. T-pins (long with large heads)
6. Tape measure
7. Crochet hook (set of various sizes; usually plastic)
8. Cable stitch holder
9. Cable needles [come in different shapes & sizes; shape is a personal preference, but size (thickness) should correspond to yarn being used.]
10. Double-ended stitch holder
11. Row counter
12. Knitting needle point protectors
13. Needle guage
14. Knitting needles:
    • straight [10" (25.4cm)]
    • straight [14" (35.6cm)]
    • circular (various cord lengths)
    • double pointed

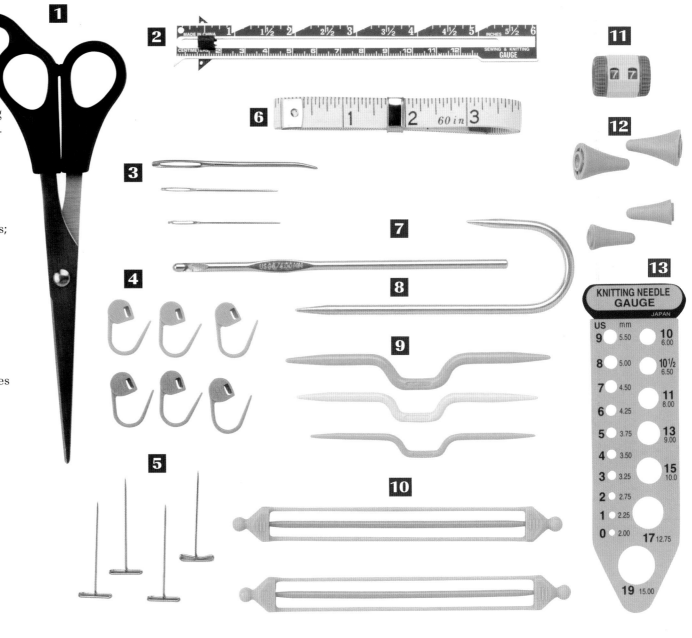

needles

Knitting needles come in a variety of sizes, types (straight, circular, double pointed), and materials (wood, plastic, aluminum), and only you can decide what works best. If you're a new knitter, you'll have to gradually build up your collection of needles.

When choosing straight needles, you'll know what size you need, but you might not be sure whether to get short [10 in. (25.4cm)] or long [14 in. (35.6cm)]. Your decision depends on the number of stitches with which you'll be working. It's no fun to knit when you've crammed too many stitches on a short needle, so if you find yourself in this predicament, invest in a longer straight or circular needle of the same size.

I've found that circular needles work well for big projects, such as blankets or throws, but they can be unwieldy for smaller projects. The knitted material eventually needs to be heavy enough to keep the plastic cord from "fighting" you.

Needles are most commonly made of wood, plastic, or aluminum. Experiment with different types as you add to your collection. Keep a copy of your inventory in your wallet so when you go shopping, you won't buy needles you already own.

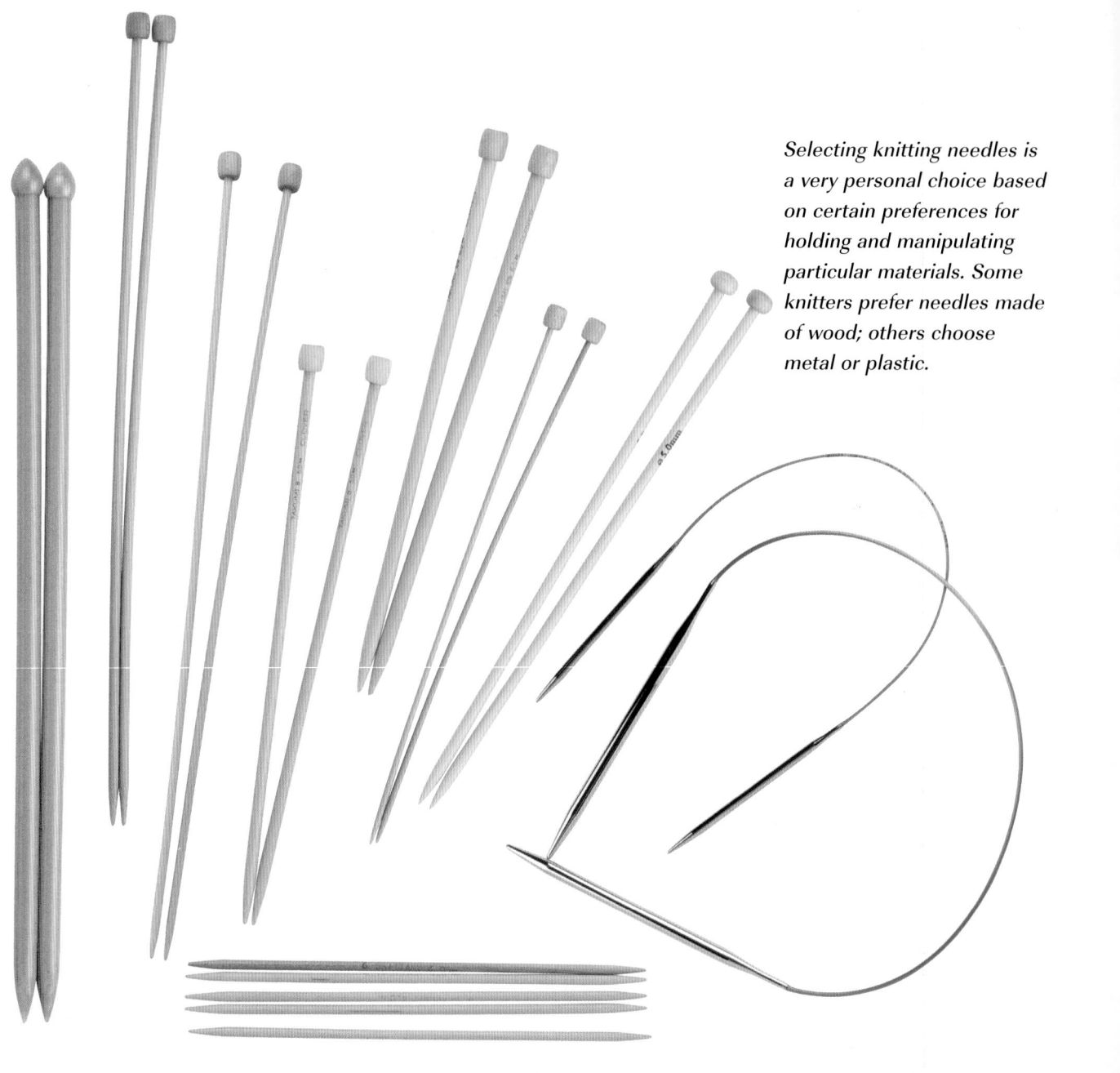

Selecting knitting needles is a very personal choice based on certain preferences for holding and manipulating particular materials. Some knitters prefer needles made of wood; others choose metal or plastic.

finding the right size needles

If you buy a pattern and a particular size needle is asked for, be sure to knit a 4 x 4-in. (10.2cm x 10.2cm) watch to ensure the right gauge. If the swatch you knit is smaller or larger than the one given in the pattern, then you'll need to adjust your needle size. Refer to details included in "Making a Gauge Swatch" on page 75 to ensure that you match the pattern gauge.

Used	US	metric (mm)	size
	0	2.00	•
	1	2.25	•
✓	2	2.75	●
✓	3	3.25	●
	4	3.50	●
✓	5	3.75	●

Used	US	metric (mm)	size
✓	6	4.25	●
✓	7	4.50	●
✓	8	5.00	●
✓	9	5.50	●
✓	10	6.00	●
✓	10½	6.50	●

Used	US	metric (mm)	size
✓	11	8.00	●
✓	13	9.00	●
✓	15	10.00	●
✓	17	12	●
✓	19	16.00	●
✓	35	19.00	●
✓	36	20	●
	50	25	●

some needle types and sizes

- straight 10" (25.4 cm)
- straight 14" (35.6 cm)
- circular 8" (20.3 cm) cord
- circular 16" (40.6 cm) cord
- circular 19" (48.3 cm) cord
- circular 29" (73.7 cm) cord
- double pointed needles

⟫TIP⟪
Whenever you buy new knitting needles, paint the end of one of them. (I use nail polish.) Then get into the habit of casting on to the marked needle. That way you will know whether you are on an odd- or even-numbered row, which is particularly helpful when following a pattern.

needles by project

Project	Size US	Size mm	Needle Type	Needle Length
Pink Gardenia Pin	10	(6mm)	straight	10" (25.4cm)
Lacy Choker	9	(5.5mm)	straight	10" (25.4cm)
Classic Beret	7	(4.5mm)	circ	16" (40.6cm)
	7	(4.5mm)	dpns	7-8" (17.8-20.3cm)
Three-Strand Necklace	5	(3.75mm)	straight	10" (25.4cm)
	9	(5.5m)	circ	16" (40.6cm)
Ruffled Scarf	10	(6mm)	circ	36" (91.4cm) cord min.
Extra-Long Flirty Scarf	17	(12mm)	straight	14" (35.6cm)
Coral and Gray Cowl Neck	7	(4.5mm)	straight,	14" (35.6cm)
	10	(6mm)	straight	10" (25.4cm)
	11	(8mm)	straight	10" (25.4cm)
	13	(9mm)	straight	10" (25.4cm)
	15	(10mm)	straight	10" (25.4cm)
	17	(12mm)	straight	14" (35.6cm)
Muffler w/Fur Pom-Poms	10	(6mm)	straight	14" (35.6cm)
Chenille Collar	11	(8mm)	straight	14" (35.6cm)
Bronze Collar w/Pin Accent	10	(6mm)	straight	14" (35.6cm)
	13	(9mm)	straight	14" (35.6cm)
	15	(10mm)	straight	14" (35.6cm)
	17	(12mm)	straight	14" (35.6cm)
	19	(16mm)	straight	14" (35.6cm)
	3	(3.25mm)	straight	14" (35.6cm)
	5	(3.75mm)	straight	14" (35.6cm)
Elegant Black Cuff	7	(4.5mm)	straight	10" (25.4cm)
Eyelash Beaded Cuff	7	(4.5mm)	straight	10" (25.4cm)

Project	Size US	Size mm	Needle Type	Needle Length
Beaded Cuff w/Beaded Fringe	5	(3.75mm)	straight	10" (25.4cm)
Mini Shawl Collar	10	(6mm)	straight	14" (35.6cm)
Extra-Chunky Ponchette	13	(9mm)	straight	14" (35.6cm)
Lacy Shrug	7	(4.5mm)	straight	14" (35.6cm)
w/Fur Collar and Cuffs	10	(6.5mm)	straight	14" (35.6cm)
	11	(8mm)	straight	14" (35.6cm)
	13	(9mm)	straight	14" (35.6cm)
	15	(10mm)	straight	14" (35.6cm)
	17	(12mm)	straight	14" (35.6cm)
	35	(19mm)	straight	14" (35.6cm)
Open-Weave Ponchette	35	(19mm)	straight	14" (35.6cm)
Faux Fur Capelet	11	(8mm)	straight	14" (35.6cm)
Ballet Sweater	8	(5mm)	straight	14" (35.6cm)
	36	(20mm)	straight	14" (35.6cm)
	8	(5mm)	straight	12" (30.5cm)
	8	(5mm)	dpns	7" (17.8cm)
Cummerbund	7	(4.5mm)	straight	14" (35.6cm)
	9	(5.5mm)	straight	14" (35.6cm)
Felted Belt w/Beaded Trim	2	(2.75mm)	straight	10" (25.4cm)
Vintage Pink Belt	2	(2.75mm)	straight	10" (25.4cm)
Cabled Armlets	7	(4.5mm)	straight	10" (25.4cm)
	3	(3.25mm)	straight	10" (25.4cm)
Fingerless Gloves	6	(4mm)	straight	16" (40.6 cm)
	5	(3.75mm)	dpns	4" (10.2cm)
Chunky Purse	13	(9mm)	straight	14" (35.6cm)

gauge

Have you heard the cautionary tale about the negligent knitter who began making a sweater for her little girl but ended up giving it to her linebacker brother? If only she had taken the time to make a gauge swatch!

Taking the time to make a gauge swatch before beginning a project seems, quite frankly, a bother, which is why so many knitters skip it. However, if you care at all about the final size of your project, you should complete this first step of the process. Remind yourself of the adage "Better safe than sorry" when you are tempted to omit this step.

It is also important to measure stitches and rows accurately; remember, fractions count. When multiplied over an entire garment, fractions of stitches and rows make a significant size difference.

If you knit a swatch that doesn't match the pattern gauge, you'll need to adjust the size of your needles. (Don't try to adjust the tension of your knitting.) If your swatch is larger, try smaller-sized needles; conversely, if your swatch is too small, switch to bigger needles. Keep at it until you find needles that will give you the correct gauge measurements. You'll be glad you did.

making a gauge swatch

Knit a swatch that is larger than the gauge measurements so that you can easily place the ruler or measuring tape along sts vertically (to count rows) and horizontally (to count sts). Make sure the fabric is lying flat. It helps to use a pin or knitting needle to point to each st as you count. Double-check your results.

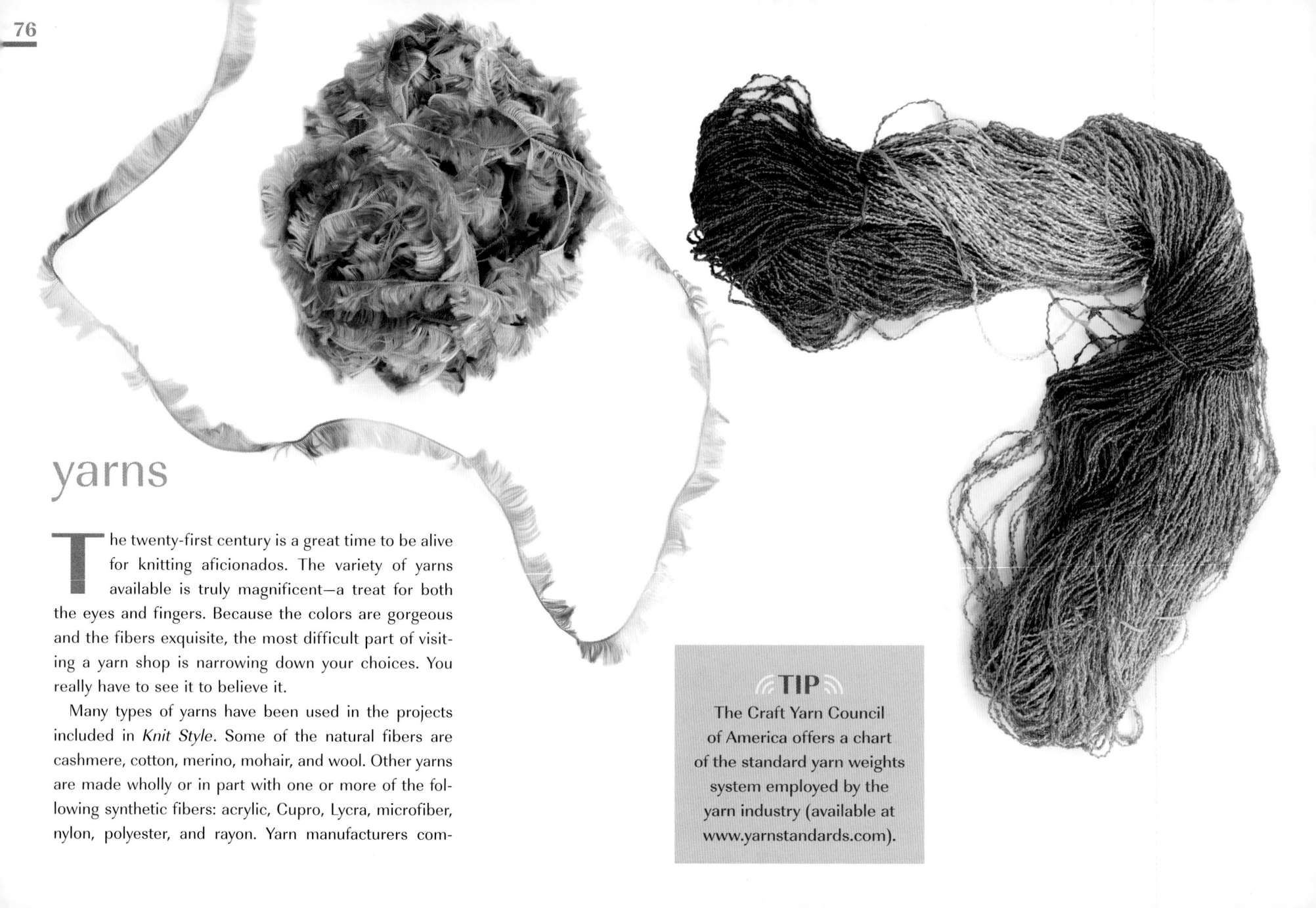

yarns

The twenty-first century is a great time to be alive for knitting aficionados. The variety of yarns available is truly magnificent—a treat for both the eyes and fingers. Because the colors are gorgeous and the fibers exquisite, the most difficult part of visiting a yarn shop is narrowing down your choices. You really have to see it to believe it.

Many types of yarns have been used in the projects included in *Knit Style*. Some of the natural fibers are cashmere, cotton, merino, mohair, and wool. Other yarns are made wholly or in part with one or more of the following synthetic fibers: acrylic, Cupro, Lycra, microfiber, nylon, polyester, and rayon. Yarn manufacturers com-

TIP

The Craft Yarn Council of America offers a chart of the standard yarn weights system employed by the yarn industry (available at www.yarnstandards.com).

monly combine natural and synthetic fibers to produce yarns that are both practical and beautiful.

Some knitting purists limit themselves to yarns made totally from natural fibers; in my opinion, they're denying themselves some fabulous yarns. Yarn producers are constantly improving existing products and developing new ones.

Another way to categorize yarn is by texture. We have used the following textures for our projects: chenille, eyelash, fuzzy, faux fur, metallic, ribbon, "suede," and thick and thin. Sometimes I knit with two or more strands of different yarns or use them separately in the same garment.

Finally, the Craft Yarn Council of America offers a chart of the standard yarn weights system employed by the yarn industry.

Yarns are given a weight number, which should appear on the label. With this information, you can find out the needle size recommended for this yarn. Also, if you find a pattern but want to try it in a different yarn, it's a good idea to substitute with a similar weight yarn. The table below illustrates a commonly-used weight system.

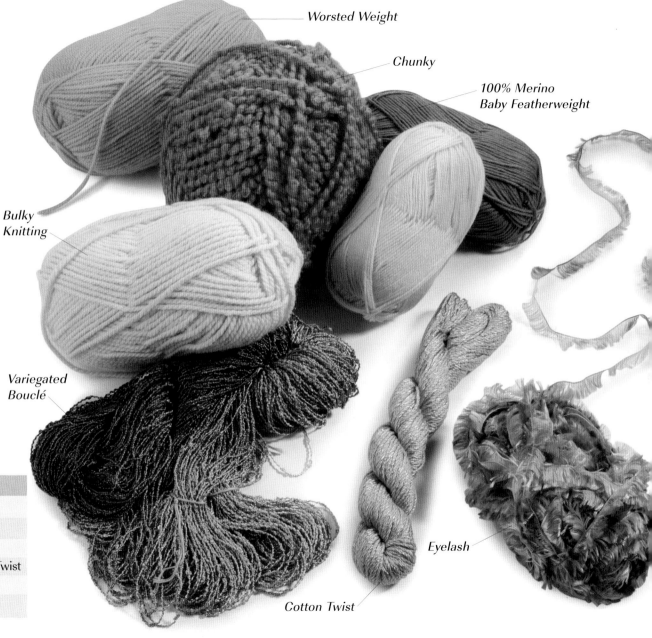

Worsted Weight

Chunky

100% Merino
Baby Featherweight

Bulky
Knitting

Variegated
Bouclé

Eyelash

Cotton Twist

Weight Category	Description
Super Fine	Sock, Fingering, Baby
Fine	Sport, Baby
Light	DK, Light Worsted, Eyelash
Medium	Worsted, Afghan, Aran, Bouclé, Cotton Twist
Bulky	Chunky, Craft, Rug
Super Bulky	Bulky, Roving

yarns by project

Project	Manufacturer	Type	Color
1 Pink Gardenia Pin	Gedifra	Cubetto	#1106
	Katia	Sevilla	#54
	Muench Yarns	Touch Me	#3642
2 Lacy Choker	Artfibers	Biscotti	#15
	Artfibers	Houdini	#4
	Artfibers	Papyrus	#143
3 Classic Beret	Lion Brand	Cashmere Blend	#124
4 Three-Strand Necklace	Katia	Sevilla	#01
	Patons	Katrina	#10005
5 Ruffled Scarf	Berroco	Zen	#8222
	Katia	Sevilla	#56
	Prism	Bon Bon	#502
6 Extra-Long Flirty Scarf	Lion Brand	Landscapes	#280
	Lion Brand	Wool-Ease Chunky	#140
	Lion Brand	Wool-Ease Chunky	#133
7 Coral and Gray Cowl-Neck	Feza	Kid Mohair	#203
	Lion Brand	Cashmere Blend	#149
8 Muffler w/Fur Pom-Poms	Lion Brand	Wool-Ease Chunky	#135
9 Chenille Collar	Lion Brand	Chenille Thick & Quick	#146
10 Bronze Collar w/Pin Accent	Berroco	Zen	#8222
	Heirloom	Breeze	#001
	Katia	Sevilla	#17
	Lion Brand	Glitterspun	#135
	Lion Brand	Suede	#126
	Knitting Fever	Flutter	#01
11 Elegant Black Cuff	Lion Brand	Lion Wool	#153

Project	Manufacturer	Type	Color
12 Eyelash Beaded Cuff	Artfibers	Papyrus	#14
	Katia	Sevilla	#02
	Trendsetter	Eyelash	#5
13 Beaded Cuff w/Beaded Fringe	Katia	Sevilla	#17
14 Mini Shawl Collar	Lion Brand	Wool-Ease Chunky	#133
15 Extra-Chunky Ponchette	Lion Brand	Landscapes	#271
	Lion Brand	Wool-Ease Worsted Weight	#139
16 Lacy Shrug w/ Fur Collar and Cuffs	Berroco	Suede	#3751
	Tahki S. Charles	Muse	#14
17 Open-Weave Ponchette	Katia	Ola	#3
	Katia	Sevilla	#01
18 Faux Fur Capelet	Lion Brand	Fun Fur	#153
	Lion Brand	Fun Fur	#191
19 Ballet-Style Sweater	Lion Brand	Cashmere Blend	#101
	Lion Brand	Fur	
20 Cummerbund Belt w/Tassel Ties	Berroco	Zen	#8222
	Katia	Sevilla	#56
	Lion Brand	Wool-Ease Worsted Weight	#123
	Prism	Bon Bon	# 502
	Victoria Fils Anny Blatt	Celeste	#156
21 Felted Belt w/Beaded Trim	Lion Brand	Lion Wool	#153
22 Vintage Pink Belt	Filatura Di Crosa	Zara	#1510
23 Cabled Armlets	Lion Brand	Cashmere Blend	#105
24 Fingerless Gloves	Filatura Di Crosa	Multicolor	#3053
	Kertzer	Truffles	#2144
25 Chunky Purse	Bouton d'Or	Norma	#050
	Colinette	Point Five	#89

yarns by manufacturer

Manufacturer	Yarn Type	Color	Project
Artfibers	"Biscotti"	burnt orange (#15)	Lacy Choker
	"Houdini"	green/brown/bronze/gold (#4)	Lacy Choker
	"Papyrus"	purple (#14)	Lacy Choker
			Eyelash Beaded Cuff
Berroco	"Suede"	strawberry (#3751)	Lacy Shrug w/Fur Collar and Cuffs
	"Zen"	acid green (#8222)	Ruffled Scarf
			Bronze Collar w/Pin Accent
			Cummerbund Belt w/Tassel Ties
Bouton d'Or	"Norma"	white (#050)	Chunky Purse
Colinette	"Point Five"	white, multi (#89)	Chunky Purse
Feza	"Kid Mohair"	coral (#203)	Coral and Gray Cowl Neck
Filatura Di Crosa	"Multicolor"	garnet mix (#3053)	Fingerless Gloves
	"Zara"	pink (#1510)	Vintage Pink Belt
Gedifra	"Cubetto"	pink/orange/purple mix (#1106)	Pink Gardenia Pin
Heirloom	"Breeze"	white (#001)	Bronze Collar w/Pin Accent
Katia	"Ola"	off-white (#3)	Three-Strand Necklace
			Open Weave Ponchette
	"Sevilla"	black (#02):	Eyelash Beaded Cuff
		bronze (#17):	Bronze Collar w/Pin Accent
			Beaded Cuff w/Beaded Fringe
		cantelope (#54):	Pink Gardenia Pin
		lime green(#56):	Ruffled Scarf
			Cummerbund Belt w/Tassel Ties
		white (#01):	Three-Strand Necklace
			Open Weave Ponchette
Kertzer	"Truffles"	garnet (#2144)	Fingerless Gloves

yarns by manufacturer

Manufacturer	Yarn Type	Color	Project
Knitting Fever	"Flutter"	white eyelash (#01)	Pink Gardenia Pin
Lion Brand	"Cashmere Blend"	Camel (#124)	Classic Beret
		Charcoal (#149)	Coral and Gray Cowl Neck
		Light Blue (#105)	Cabled Armlets
		Light Pink (#101)	Ballet-Style Sweater
	"Chenille Thick & Quick"	Dark Purple (#146)	Chenille Collar
	"Fun Fur"	Black (#153)	Faux Fur Capelet
		Violet (#191)	Faux Fur Capelet
	"Glitterspun"	Bronze (#135)	Bronze Collar w/Pin Accent
	"Landscapes"	Rasp. Patch (#280)	Extra Long Flirty Scarf
		Rose Garden (#271)	Extra-Chunky Ponchette
	"Lion Wool"	black (#153)	Elegant Black Cuff
			Felted Belt w/Beaded Trim
	"Suede"	Coffee (#126)	Bronze Collar w/Pin Accent
	"Tiffany Article 260"	Light Pink (#101)	Ballet-Style Sweater
	"Wool-Ease Chunky"	Deep Rose (#140)	Extra-Long Flirty Scarf
		Pumpkin (#630-133)	Extra-Long Flirty Scarf
			Mini Shawl Collar
		Spice (#135)	Muffler w/ Fur Pom-Poms
	"Wool-Ease Worsted Weight"	Dark Rose Heather (#139)	Extra-Chunky Ponchette
		Seaspray (#123)	Cummerbund Belt w/Tassel Ties
Muench Yarns	"Touch Me"	salmon (#3642)	Pink Gardenia Pin
Patons	"Katrina"	white (#10005)	Three-Strand Necklace
Prism	"Bon Bon"	celery (#502)	Ruffled Scarf
			Cummerbund Belt w/Tassel Ties
Tahki S. Charles	"Muse"	strawberry, multi (#14)	Lacy Shrug w/Fur Collar and Cuffs
Trendsetter	"Eyelash"	black (#5)	Eyelash Beaded Cuff
Victoria Fils Anny Blatt	"Celeste"	teal (#156)	Cummerbund Belt w/Tassel Ties

knitting techniques

every one you need to begin

K nitting is a creative process that is based on several fundamental techniques. Those techniques are illustrated and explained in this section, a kind of "Knitting 101," dedicated to demystifying

the methods you need if you are to proceed from casting on those first stitches on your needles (using that

scrumptious yarn that inspired you in the first place), to actually finishing the chosen knitted accessory that

you will be happy to wear or give. The steps in the knitting process should be fun, even exhilarating, and

often they are both; however, there are times when a particular direction may be unfamiliar to you, or con-

fusing, and you will need some help figuring things out. Here, you will find each of the basic knitting tech-

niques explained in simple language and illustrated by concise photographs showing the up-close details

in each step in the knitting process. In addition, the "Textured Stitches" section will inspire you to try new

patterns. Finally, there is a handy table of abbreviations to help streamline the decoding process, making

all the patterns easy to follow.

abbreviations

acrs	=	across
alt	=	alternate
beg	=	begin/beginning
bo	=	bind off
C	=	cable
CN	=	cable needle
co	=	cast on
cont	=	continue
dec	=	decrease
foll	=	following
g st	=	garter stitch
inc	=	increase
k	=	knit
k2tog	=	knit 2 sts together
k-wise	=	knitwise
LN	=	left needle
M1	=	make 1 stitch

how to use this section *

Knit Style is designed specifically with you, the knitter, in mind. Its unique format— spiral-bound, easel-style, makes "hands-free" knitting possible. Now you can follow the directions for any technique featured in *Knit Style* while you are knitting. Find the technique you are interested in, open to the page, and stand up the book with the page

facing you. Knit as directed, feeling free to check your work by referring to the photographs as you knit. When the directions continue on the next page, rotate the book and continue following the directions. If you need to turn the page over, orient the new page so the text faces you. The spiral will make it easy to flip the page over.

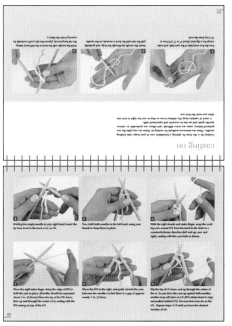

* Stand up the book and read here first.

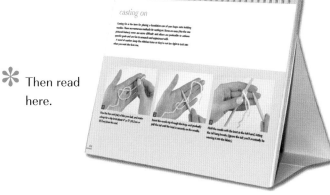

* Then read here.

N	=	needle
p	=	purl
p2tog	=	purl 2 sts together
p3tog	=	purl 3 sts together
patt	=	pattern
psso	=	pass slipped st over
p-wise	=	purlwise
rem	=	remaining
rep	=	repeat
R	=	row
RN	=	right needle
RS	=	right side of garment
skpo	=	slip 1, knit 1, pass slipped st over
sl	=	slip
ssk/ssp	=	slip, slip, knit/slip, slip, purl
st(s)	=	stitch(es)
st st	=	stockinette stitch
strd(s)	=	strand(s)
tbl	=	through back of loop
tog	=	together
WS	=	wrong side of garment
yn	=	yarn
YN#	=	specific yarn used in garment
yo	=	yarn over needle

symbols

[ ]	=	groups a sequence of directions
*	=	marks beg of sequential directions, usually repeated to end of row

casting on

Casting On is the term for placing a foundation row of yarn loops onto knitting needles. There are numerous methods for casting on. Some are easy (like the one pictured below); some are more difficult; and others are preferable to achieve specific goals and are fun to research and experiment with.

A word of caution: keep the stitches loose so they're not too tight to knit into when you work the first row.

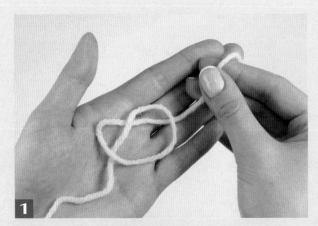

1 Free the free end (tail) of the yarn ball, and make a loop for a slip knot about 4 or 5 in. (10.2 or 12.7cm) from the end.

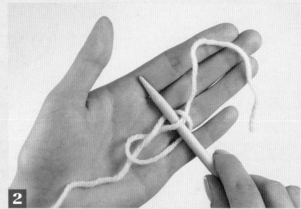

2 Insert the needle tip through the loop, and gradually pull the tail until the knot is securely on the needle.

3 Hold the needle with the knot in the left hand, letting the tail hang loosely. (Ignore the tail; you'll eventually be weaving it into the fabric.)

4 Holding the empty needle in your right hand, insert the tip from the front to the back of st on the LN.

5 Now hold both needles in the left hand, using your thumb to keep them in place.

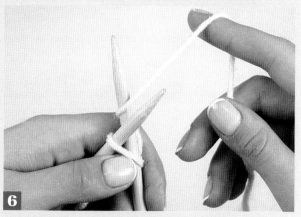

6 With the right thumb and index finger, wrap the working yarn around the RN from the back to the front in a counterclockwise direction (left and up, over and right), ending with the yarn held as shown.

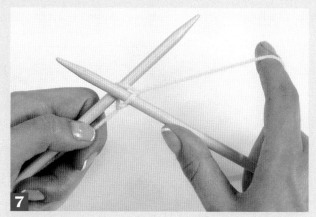

7 Place the right index finger along the edge of the RN to hold the yarn in place. [Needles should be separated about ¼ in. (0.6cm).] Move the tip of the RN down, then up and through the center of the st, ending with the RN resting on top of the LN.

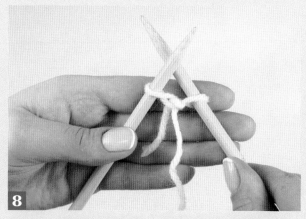

8 Move the RN to the right, and gently stretch the yarn between the needles so that there is a gap of approximately 1 in. (2.5cm).

9 Dip the tip of the LN down and up through the center of the st. As you draw the yarn up against both needles, another loop will form on the LN (the RN rotates back to original position behind the LN). You now have two sts on the LN. Repeat steps 4–9 until you have the desired number of sts.

knit stitch

Now that you have a foundation row of stitches, you are ready to knit. The first order of business is mastering the knit stitch. You'll be happy to discover that many of the steps are the same as for casting on.

Most new knitters pull their stitches too tight. Concentrate on pulling the yarn so that it's taut enough to rest snugly but not tightly against the needles. Adjust the tension so that you can insert the right needle into the stitch and maneuver it easily. As with any new skill, any awkwardness will disappear as you practice until your motions are fluid and automatic.

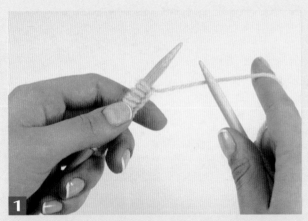

1 Always begin a row holding the needle with sts on it in your left hand; the first st should be about 1 in. (2.5cm) away from the needle tip. Hold the empty needle along with the working yarn in your right hand.

2 Insert the tip of the RN into st from front to back, ending behind the LN (the same motion as in step 4 of "Casting On").

3 With your right thumb and index finger, hold the working yarn to the right and slightly behind [approximately 2 in. (5.1cm) away from] the needles. Wrap the yarn around the RN from back to front in a counterclockwise direction (left and up, over and right), ending with the yarn held as shown (as in step 6 of "Casting On" on page 84).

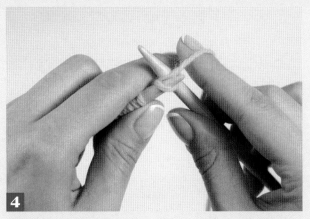

4

Place your right index finger along the edge of the RN to hold yarn in place. [Needles should be separated by about ¼ in. (0.6cm).]

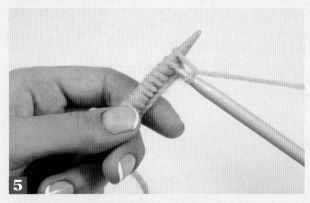

5

Move the tip of the RN down, then up and through the center of the st, ending with the RN resting on top of the LN (as in step 7 of "Casting On").

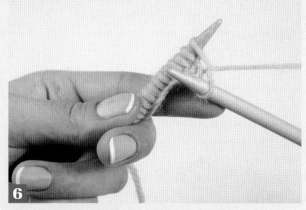

6

Slide the RN toward the tip of the LN until loop drops off—one loop only. You've accomplished your first knit stitch.

7

Continue following steps 2–6 until you have knitted every st on the needle. Then turn your work so that the needle with sts is in your left hand. (Remember the rule: always begin a row holding the needle with sts in your left hand and the empty needle in your right.) After you've knit several rows, your fabric should look like the photo. When every stitch of every row is knitted, the resulting pattern is called garter stitch.

purl stitch

The purl stitch is the other essential component of most textured stitch patterns. Though the number of motions is the same as for the knit stitch, there are two main differences: the position of the working yarn in relation to the needles and the manner in which the right needle is inserted into the stitch on the left needle. That's it.

If you've ever played tennis, you know that the two basic strokes are the forehand and backhand. Chances are that you find performing one of these strokes a bit easier, more fluidly, than the other. But to the untrained observer, the purpose of both these strokes is the same—to score points. Knitting and purling are analogous in that they are the two basic "strokes," and both have the same purpose—to create stitches, which collectively form fabric. Most novice knitters feel a bit more proficient with either knitting or purling, but after a while the difference is hardly noticeable. So if you feel a bit clumsy at first and find it hard to remember what's what, rest assured that you will eventually knit and purl with ease.

Instead of holding the yarn behind the needles as you do when you are knitting, hold the yarn in front. And instead of inserting the tip of the RN from the front to the back of the st on the LN, insert the needle from the back to front.

2

Loop the yarn around the tip of the RN in a counter-clockwise direction (left and up, over and right).

3

Rest the LN against the left index finger as you slide the tip of the RN down and through the center of the st on the LN, ending with the RN behind the LN. Use the left index finger to slide the loop toward the tip of the needle until it drops off.

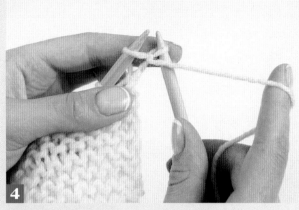

4

You've completed your first purl st and now have a loop on the RN. Repeat the steps until you have purled each st on the needle.

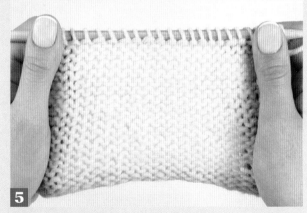

5

This photo shows the "purl side" of the stockinette stitch pattern. Notice that the texture is bumpy and the sts appear to undulate horizontally. More simply, they look like a succession of little hills. Knit several rows, and your fabric should look like the photo above.

stockinette stitch

Stockinette stitch (st st) is produced by knitting the odd-numbered rows and purling the even-numbered ones. The knitted side is flat, and the purled side is bumpy (looks like the garter stitch). When a knitted piece is worked entirely in st st, the edges of the piece will curl. This is not a problem if the curl is desired or if the piece will be sewn to another one. But if you want an item to lie flat, knit a seed-stitch or ribbed border to eliminate the curl.

⟨ TIP ⟩

Use a row counter; it will save you lots of "do-overs." Get in the habit of recording a row as soon as you finish it. If you are following a pattern or creating a textured stitch, you must know what row you are on.

1 This is the knit side—often considered the right side (RS)—of st st. The texture is flat, and the sts look like Vs. If you are holding your knitting in your left hand and this side is facing you, k the next row.

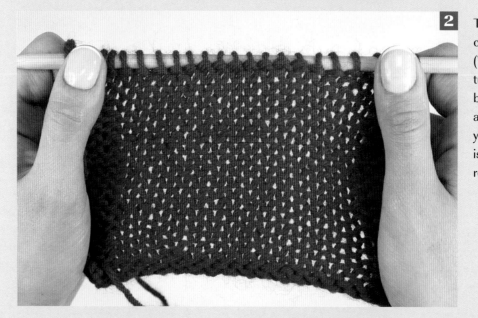

2 This is the purl side—often considered the wrong side (WS)—of the st st. The texture is bumpy and resembles the garter stitch. If you are holding your knitting in your left hand and this side is facing you, p the next row.

ribbing

Rib patterns are created by alternating a specific number of knit and purl stitches within the same row. They give the knitted piece an elasticity useful in a variety of contexts where stretchability is desired: waists, necks, and wrists of sweaters, hats, socks, etc. There is no set ribbon pattern, although a 1/1 or 2/2 rib is most commonly used for borders: But the rib stitch isn't just for borders; its attractiveness and multiple variations make it equally appropriate for an entire garment.

⟨TIP⟩
Bind off ribbed stitches
in pattern (k the k's
and p the p's)
in order to
maintain elasticity.

1 This photo is of a 2/2 rib pattern, which is created by knitting 2 sts, then purling 2 sts, continuing in the same sequence, until the row is completed. From then on, you will k the knitted sts and p the purled sts. Don't forget to move the working yarn back and forth between the needles as you alternate between k's and p's; keep the yarn behind the needles when knitting and in front when purling.

2 Here, the 2/2 rib pattern is stretched out to reveal the texture. The k sts appear raised while the p sts look recessed. Left unstretched, the p sts are barely visible.

picking up stitches

Casting on new stitches isn't the only way to add stitches to a needle. Another way is to pick up stitches along a bound-off edge with a knitting needle. (This method is often used to add a border.) Because you want the addition to blend seamlessly, start picking up stitches at the very bottom and end at the top. Don't pick up loops randomly; make sure you select a loop from each stitch along the bound-off edge of the fabric to which you are adding.

᚛TIP᚜
If at all possible, don't put knitting down in the middle of a row; the chance of losing stitches increases.

1 To begin, examine the first st along the edge to find the most accessible loop. Then, entering from the top, insert the needle and slide the st about 1 in. (2.5cm) from the needle tip.

2 Wrap the yarn across the other needle in the right hand, leaving the usual 4-in. (10.2cm) tail.

3 Pull the yarn through the st on the LN with the RN.

4 You've now got 1 picked-up st on the RN.

5 Insert the LN in the next st on the piece edge.

6 Wrap the yarn around the RN; then pull the yarn through the st on the LN. Continue picking up and knitting loops from each st on the main fabric to end up with a new row of "live" sts. When you have completed picking up all the loops, you can continue.

increasing stitches, yarn over

The two most common methods of shaping knitted fabric are increasing and decreasing the number of stitches during the knitting process.

Although there are many ways of increasing the number of stitches on a needle, the Yarn Over (yo) is one that is often found in knitting patterns, probably because it is very simple to do and produces an eyelet for an open, lacy look.

1 When you arrive at the place in the knit row that calls for a yo, wrap the yarn around the needle as if to k, then k the next st. This results in an extra loop on the RN.

2 In the next row, which is purled, you will arrive at the extra loop you made in the previous row. Treat it as a regular stitch, and purl it. You have now increased the stitch count by one.

increasing between a stitch

Many knitters feel that increasing between a stitch (also called Make One and abbreviated M1) is one of the best methods for adding a stitch because it blends so well into the surrounding stitches.

1 When you arrive at the place in the knit row that calls for increasing between a st (M1), stretch the needles apart slightly and locate the horizontal bar between the sts. Insert the tip of the LN from the front to the back under the bar, and lift onto the needle as shown.

2 Insert the RN through the back of the loop, and k. You have increased the st count by one.

3 On the p side, lift the bar onto the LN the same way, but p the st through the back loop to make the new st.

decreasing stitches, ssk/ssp

Like increasing, decreasing the number of stitches on the needle is used to shape a garment. And like increasing, there is more than one way to accomplish it.

One of the most popular ways to decrease is called slip, slip, knit (ssk) on the knit side or slip, slip, purl (ssp) on the purl side.

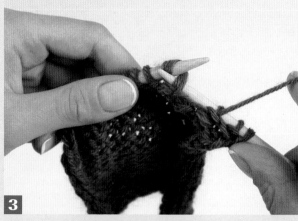

1 On the k side, when you arrive at the place where a decrease is called for (ssk), slip the next 2 sts as if you were knitting, one at a time, from the LN to the RN.

2 Insert the LN into the fronts of the 2 sts, and k them together. Your st count has been reduced by one.

3 On the p side, when you arrive at the place where a decrease is called for (ssp), slip the next 2 stitches as if you were knitting, one at a time, from the LN to the RN. Insert the LN through the back of the loops, and p them together. Again, your st count has been reduced by one.

decreasing stitches, knit/purl 2 together

Another commonly used method for decreasing the number of stitches on a needle is called Knit (or Purl) Two Together. The abbreviations in knitting patterns are usually k2tog (p2tog).

Unlike the ssk/ssp method, which produces stitches that slant to the left, this method results in stitches that slant right. Because of the opposite slants, you'll often find that the ssk/ssp method is used on one side and the k2tog is used on the other side of a symmetrical garment.

1 On the knit side, when you reach the place for the decrease, knit two stitches together as if they were one.

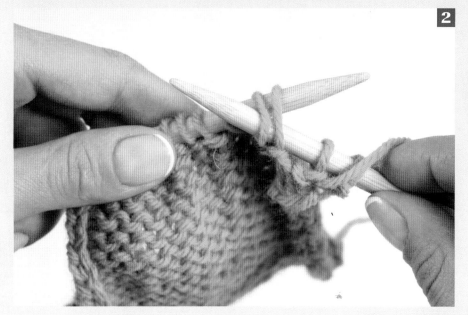

2 On the purl side, when you reach the place for the decrease, purl two stitches together as if they were one.

slipping stitches

Being directed to slip (sl) one or more stitches is quite common. There are two ways to slip a stitch—knitwise (k-wise) and purlwise (p-wise). Basically, when you slip a stitch, you are transfer-ring it from the left to the right needle without knitting or purling it.

TIP

If you are directed to slip more than one stitch—sl2, sl3, etc.—it is best to slip them one at a time rather than trying to "spear" them as a group.

1 slipping knitwise

To sl st k-wise, insert the RN into the first st on the LN as you would for a k st, but instead of knitting, merely transfer it to the RN.

2 slipping purlwise

To sl st p-wise, insert the RN into the first st on the LN as if you would for a p st, but instead of purling, merely transfer it to the RN.

joining in new yarn

Joining new yarn to the working yarn is as easy as tying a knot. Even though it is tempting to keep knitting until a ball is used up, plan to add new yarn only at the beginning of a row; if done anywhere else, the knot and tails will be noticeable. It is definitely worth sacrificing a bit of yarn to produce an attractive garment.

Tie the new yarn to the working yarn, leaving a tail of about 4 in. (10.2cm). Make a knot as close to the needle as possible—secure but not too tight.

❮TIP❯

When purchasing multiple balls/skeins of yarn for a project, make sure they are from the same dye lot. Variations among dye lots can be significant.

Weave in yarn tails as you knit rather than waiting until you're done with the garment. It's much less tedious this way.

cable stitch

Cables look difficult, but they're actually easy to make. Cables come in many varieties with two common denominators: they are made from an even number of stitches, and the second half of the cable is knitted before the first half, usually on the right side of the work.

A cable needle (CN) makes it possible to knit the second half of a cable first. Unlike regular knitting needles, which have only one point and come in numerous sizes, cable needles have points on both ends and are basically thin, thick, and thicker. Select one that roughly corresponds to the size of the knitting needles you are using. Most commonly, cable needles are made from aluminum or plastic and are shaped like a hook or have a notch in the center. Fortunately, cable needles aren't as costly as regular needles, so you can experiment to see which kind suits you best.

Before beginning your project, practice with the cable needle until you feel comfortable using it. The key to making cables successfully is to be scrupulous about following the pattern. Using a row counter is a must. I've also found it helpful to use stitch markers to identify cable sections, so I don't inadvertently ignore them. One caution: don't be concerned if you find the row after the cable row a bit difficult to knit; this is normal and due to the twisting of the stitches.

Two types of cables are shown in these photos: the left (front) cable and the right (back) cable. Cables can be made from any number of stitches (as long as the number is even) and can be as short or tall as desired. The generic designation left (front) means that when the cable needle is held in front of the work, the resulting cables will "climb" to the left. In a right (back) cable, created by placing the cable needle behind the work, the cables climb right.

left front cable

1 In a cable pattern, the row in which the sts are transferred from the LN to the CN is called the cable row. After transferring the required number of sts to the CN, let the CN hang horizontally in front of the work.

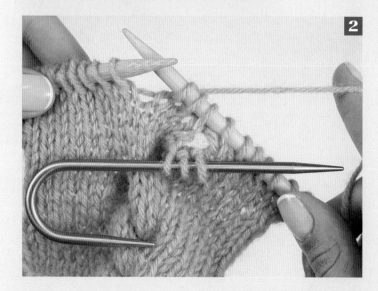

2 K the required number of sts from the LN.

3 There are two ways to complete this next step. K the sts directly from the CN as shown, or transfer the sts from the CN back to the LN and continue knitting as usual.

4 After completing several sets of the cable pattern, your fabric should look like the photo at the left. Notice the cables curving to the left.

TIP

Learning to knit a cable
may take some practice.
Be patient and enjoy
the challenge.

right back cable

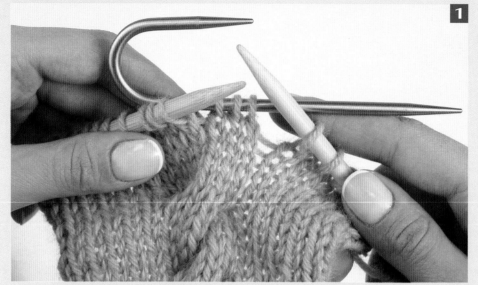

1 The only difference between right (back) and left (front) cables is where the CN is kept once the sts have been transferred to it—in front or in back of the work. To begin the right (back) cable, follow the directions for the left (front) cable, but place the CN behind your work.

2 K the required number of sts from the LN.

TIP

The key to making cables successfully is to be scrupulous about following the pattern. Using a row counter is a must.

3 There are two ways to complete this next step. K the sts directly from the CN as shown, or transfer the sts from the CN back to the LN and continue knitting as usual.

4 After completing several sets of the cable pattern, your fabric should look like the photo to the left. Notice the cables curving to the right.

recovering a dropped stitch

You've no doubt seen knitting with unattractive holes caused by a knitter who ignored a dropped stitch and continued on, forgetting to go back to fix it.

Using needle guards goes a long way toward preventing dropped stitches, but despite their best efforts, most knitters face this problem sooner or later. Consequently, you should know how to recover a dropped stitch. If you drop a stitch but don't notice it for a while, you may be better off sliding the stitches off the needle and undoing rows until you reach the mistake. This can be risky if your yarn is slippery and the loops disappear as soon as they come off the needle. If this is the case, choose the safer option of leaving the stitches on the needle and undoing them one at a time.

As you can see from the photo, a dropped stitch isn't pretty. Address the problem as soon as you notice it.

A crochet hook is a handy tool for recovering dropped stitches, so keep one in your knitting bag. Find the run-away loop, and grab it from below with the hook as shown. Now hook the horizontal bar above it, and draw it toward you through center of the loop. The bar has now become the loop.

If the loop is on the same row as the rest of your knitting, lift it back onto the LN and continue. If you aren't at the top yet, continue the procedure in step 2 until you reach the top row.

binding off

Binding off is like crossing the finish line after a marathon—if you have gotten this far, you know you've finished your knitting.

1

Beg in the bind-off row by knitting the first 2 sts. Insert the tip of the LN into the front of the first st (on the right) as shown.

2

Lift the st on the LN over the other stitch and completely over the tip of the RN, allowing it to drop off completely. Don't worry—your stitch hasn't been dropped, just bound off.

3

When you come to the last st, snip off the working yarn [leaving a 4-in. (10.1 cm) tail]; then elongate the st a bit so you can slide it off the needle easily without losing the loop. Grab the loop, and guide the end of the tail through the center. Continue drawing the yarn through the loop until it is up against the fabric; then knot it securely. Don't make a knot too soon, or you'll stretch out the sts.

finishing: weaving in ends

Weaving in ends (tails) is part of the finishing process. To avoid the tedium of dealing with all of them after you've completed the project, weave in the ends during the knitting process. Occasionally, you'll work with a yarn that doesn't want to stay in place; use a needle and thread to tack it down as inconspicuously as possible.

Thread a blunt-end needle with the yarn tail, and weave it along the edge of the fabric as shown. For extra security, reverse the direction and weave another 1 in. (2.5cm) or so, securing the yarn in place. Cut off the excess yarn.

finishing: sewing together

Finishing techniques and the sewing stitches used to join knitted pieces are numerous. You need to be as conscientious about the finishing process as you were about the knitting. For the best result, do not omit blocking the pieces if the pattern calls for it. Blocking is usually done before sewing. Allow plenty of time for blocked pieces to dry (usually about 24 hours) before sewing them together; it will be worth the wait.

1 To join two garter st pieces, thread a blunt-end needle with the same yarn used to k. If the pieces aren't the same color (as in the photo), the selection is your choice. Even though both pieces look the same on both sides, choose the sides you want showing, and place them face up. Line up the pieces so that you can sew from one to the other, matching corresponding sts as you go.

Starting from the outside, insert the needle through the first st at the bottom of the left-hand piece. Then direct the needle over to and under the bottom st of the right-hand piece; draw the needle up from the center and out on top. Pull the yarn taut enough so that the pieces are adjoined and lie flat.

2 Continue working up and side-to-side between the pieces while drawing the yarn tightly enough to eliminate gaps but not so tightly that the seams buckle.

finishing: joining stockinette

When working with st st pieces, the k side (flat texture) is usually considered the RS. After threading a needle with matching yarn, align the pieces. Begin with the first st at the bottom, and work up to the last st at the top. The photo at left shows what part of the st to pierce as you sew. Again, draw the yarn tightly enough to eliminate gaps but not so tightly that the seams buckle.

TIP
Wax your thread when beading or sewing on buttons because it reduces tangling and makes the thread sturdier.

When joining shoulder seams, you are working with bound-off edges. Arrange the pieces to be joined with the RS facing you and aligned side by side. Again, start at the bottom and work to the top, moving the needle from one piece to the other as you sew the corresponding sts tog. The key to sewing bound-off edges tog is to not work with the bound-off sts; instead, work with the sts immediately next to the bound-off sts. For the blue piece, you would work the first row of sts to the left of its edge; for the purple piece, choose the sts immediately to the right of its edge.

⌒TIP⌒
Blocking

STEAM: Lay the piece WS down on a padded surface, and cover it with a pressing cloth. Press lightly with a steam iron. Set the iron down carefully; do not drag the iron as this will stretch the piece. This method will allow you to manipulate the fabric and achieve greater length or width if desired. It will also set the stitches and even out the stitch quality for a more professional look.

STEAM LIGHTLY: Lay the piece WS down on a padded surface, and move the steam iron slowly back and forth 1 in. (2.5cm) above the piece. Do not allow the iron to touch knitted fabric. Steam will allow the knitted fabric to "blossom." Selvages and ribbings will lay flat. This method may not allow you to block pieces that are larger.

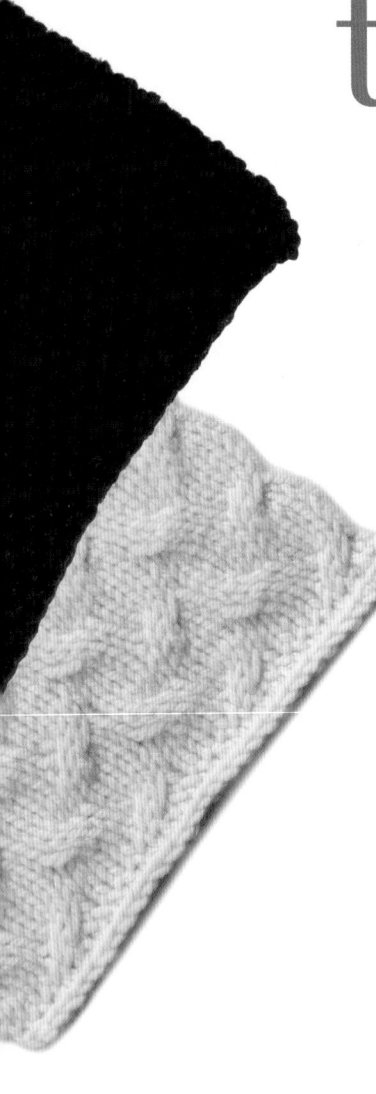

textured stitches

add variety and fun to your knitting

L et's start with the basics: the knit and purl stitches are the building blocks of knitting. A garment can be made by knitting every stitch or purling every stitch. Most garments are made by using combinations of these two stitches—which are endless.

The two basic textured stitches are garter and stockinette. Take a look at a sweater. Usually the knit side (flat texture) is the right side and the purl side (bumpy texture) is the wrong side. Contrary to what you might expect, the knit side is produced by purling and the purl side by knitting. (Don't worry if this is confusing to you; after a little experience, it won't be.)

Every stitch pattern, no matter how complex, is essentially made up of knit and purl stitches. In the stitch patterns used in this book, the odd-numbered rows are usually the same, as are the even-numbered rows. (As a general rule, odd and even rows are the reverse of each other.) Usually one row in the pattern is different from the others; it is this row that creates the unique texture.

Textured stitch patterns are developed over a specific number of rows; taken together, these rows form a set. (No stitch pattern in this book has more than an eight-row set.) The original set is repeated as often as needed to attain the desired length. In general, sets are completed before moving on to another stitch.

Although it is necessary to keep track of every row, special attention needs to be paid to the exceptional row. The other rows can often be simplified by using this guide: knit the knit stitches and purl the purl stitches. (An even shorter version to mentally say to yourself is, "Knit the knits and purl the purls.") However, some stitch patterns, like seed and moss, are created by doing the opposite: knitting the purls and purling the knits. If you take a minute to analyze a stitch pattern, you'll often find that you can apply one of these guides to help you develop the pattern efficiently.

Once you've been bitten by the knitting bug, you'll want to try new stitches. Invest in a knitting reference book, and start teaching yourself new stitch patterns. After selecting a textured stitch—at first, stick to those with fewer rows in a set—practice it until you've worked out the inevitable kinks; then incorporate it into your next knitting project. You'll discover that it's extremely gratifying to expand your stitch repertoire.

make a memory card

Making what I call a stitch memory card helps me succeed with textured stitch patterns. Following is a moss-stitch memory card:

MOSS STITCH

R1: [K1, p1] acrs
R2: [K1, p1] acrs
R3: [P1, k1] acrs
R4: [P1, k1] acrs

(Repeat rows 1–4 for pattern.)

SETS:

After having fun with fonts and colors, I print this out on a piece of card stock, which is sturdy enough to cut out and place in a paper holder. Armed with this card and my row counter, I am confident I can follow the pattern accurately. I reset my row counter after each four-row set, so I always know where I am in the pattern. (Of course, remembering to use the row counter is important if the system is to work.) To keep track of the total number of rows worked, I record each four-row set upon completion (in pencil, so I can use the card again).

Another helpful way to keep track of where you are is to color code each pair of needles. I use brightly colored nail polish to paint the cap end of one of the needles, and then I always cast on to the color-coded needle. (For circular needles, I paint one of the needles at the point where it attaches to the cord.) By using this system, I can tell at a glance whether my next row should be odd- or even-numbered. If the stitches are on the marked needle, I will begin with an odd-numbered row; conversely, if the stitches are on the unmarked needle, I will begin with an even-numbered row.

By all means, don't allow mistakes to deprive you of the pleasure of learning a new stitch pattern. If you try one without success, check another resource; often the different wording leads to that "Aha!" moment that gets you over the hurdle.

garter stitch

This stitch is used for the Chenille Collar on page 28.

The simplest textured stitch, garter is made by knitting every stitch in every row. Both sides of the work will look like the purl side of stockinette (bumpy).

All rows: K acrs.

stockinette stitch

This stitch is used for the Ballet-Style Sweater on page 52.

The workhorse of stitch patterns, stockinette is made by knitting the odd-numbered rows and purling the even-numbered rows, resulting in a knit side with a flat surface, usually considered the right side, and a purl side with a bumpy texture.

Row 1: K acrs.
Row 2: P acrs.

(Rep rows 1 and 2 for patt.)

REVERSE STOCKINETTE STITCH

This stitch is used for the Open-Weave Ponchette on page 48.

The opposite of stockinette, reverse stockinette is made by purling the odd-numbered rows and knitting the even-numbered rows.

Row 1: P acrs.
Row 2: K acrs.

(Rep rows 1 and 2 for patt.)

seed stitch

This stitch is used for the Vintage Pink Belt on page 62.

Delicate-looking when small needles and fine yarn are used, the
seed stitch lends elegance to any
knitted fabric. When longer needles and chunkier yarn are used,
the "cross hatch" texture appears
more pronounced.

(Multiple of 2 sts)

Row 1: (RS): [K1, p1] acrs.
Row 2: [P1, k1] acrs.

(Rep rows 1 and 2 for patt.)

moss stitch

This stitch is used for the Beaded Cuff With Beaded Fringe on page 38.

The "tweed" character of the moss stitch is one of its appealing characteristic features, often compared with the seed stitch. The moss stitch is noted for its discernible vertical and "crosshatch" stitches; whereas, the seed stitch has only a "crosshatch" appearance.

(Multiple of 2 sts)

Row 1: (RS): [K1, p1] acrs.
Row 2: [K1, p1] acrs.
Row 3: [P1, k1] acrs.
Row 4: [P1, k1] acrs.

(Rep rows 1–4 for patt.)

basketweave stitch

This stitch is used for the Cummerbund Belt with Tassel Ties on page 56.

The basketweave stitch produces a checkerboard appearance by alternating groups of knit and purl stitches on the same side of the work. Squares or rectangles can be made by adjusting the number of stitches and rows to attain the desired size and shape. For symmetry, boxes in all four corners should be the same stitch and size.

(Each box is 5 sts wide by 6 rows high)

Row 1: [K5, p5] acrs; end with k5.
Row 2: [P5, k5] acrs; end with p5.
Row 3: Same as row 1.
Row 4: Same as row 2.
Row 5: Same as row 1.
Row 6: Same as row 2.
Row 7: [P5, k5] acrs; end with p5.
Row 8: [K5, p5] acrs; end with k5.
Row 9: Same as row 7.
Row 10: Same as row 8.
Row 11: Same as row 7.
Row 12: Same as row 8.

(Rep rows 1–12 for patt.)

1/1 rib stitch

This stitch is used for the the Cabled Armlets on page 69.

There is no set rib pattern. After the first row of knits and purls is established, the pattern is maintained by knitting the knits and purling the purls. It's as simple as that.

The elasticity of the rib stitch makes it excellent for garment borders and areas that require stretchability. The most common pattern, a 2/2 rib, is usually found at the wrist ends and bottoms of sweaters and is created by [k2, p2] across. But the rib is not just for borders; its attractiveness and multiple variations make it equally appropriate for an entire garment.

1/1 RIB

If the fabric in the photo weren't being stretched, it would look more like the knit side of stockinette. Most other rib patterns resemble a succession of vertical rows.

Row 1: [K1, p1] acrs.
Row 2: [P1, k1] acrs.

(Rep rows 1 and 2 for patt.)

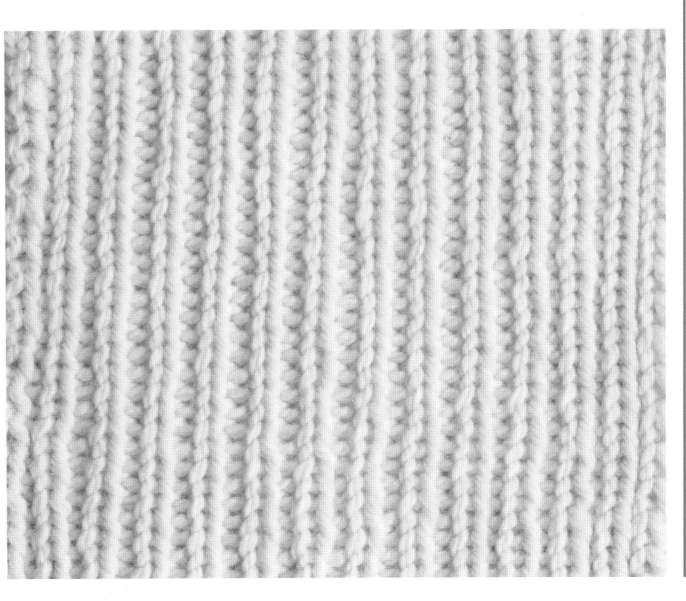

3/1 rib stitch

This stitch is used for the Extra Long Flirty Scarf on page 18.

The 3/1 rib stitch produces the appearance of wide "rails" in a knitted fabric. When chunky yarn is used, the rails have a significant rise to them. To create a more subtle look, use smaller needles and lighter-weight yarn.

Row 1: [K3, p1] acrs.
Row 2: [P3, p1] acrs.

(Rep rows 1 and 2 for patt.)

four-stitch cable and 1/1 rib combination

This stitch is used for the Cabled Armlets on page 42.

Sporty and elegant, this stitch requires some experience to do. Cable stitch patterns vary according to where the cable needle is held. If you hold the cable needle in the front, your cables will slope to the right; holding it in back results in cables that slope left.

Cable 4 Back (c4b; uses 4 consecutive sts): sl the next 2 sts onto the CN and hold them in back of the work. K2 from LN, return the sts from the CN to the LN in reverse order, being careful not to twist the sts, then k2.

(Multiple of 9 sts + 5)

Row 1: (RS): *[P1, k1] twice, p1, k4; rep from *; end p1, [k1, p1] twice.
Row 2: *[K1, p1] twice, k1, p4; rep from *; end [k1, p1] twice, k1.
Row 3: *[P1, k1] twice, p1, c4b; rep from *; end p1, [k1, p1] twice.
Row 4: Same as row 2.

(Rep rows 1–4 for patt.)

six-stitch cable stitch

This stitch is used for the Extra-Chunky Ponchette on page 42.

A more pronounced texture, this cable pattern introduces elegant "twists" or braid-like verticals on the knitted fabric.

Cable 6 Back (c6b; uses 6 consecutive sts): sl the next 3 sts onto the CN and hold them in back of the work. K3 from the LN, return the sts from the CN to the LN in reverse order, being careful not to twist the sts, then k3.

(Multiple of 11 sts + 1)

Row 1 and all odd-numbered rows: P1, [k2, p6, k2, p1] acrs.
Row 2: (RS): K1, [p2, k6, p2, k1] acrs.
Row 4: Same as row 2.
Row 6: K1, [p2, c6b, p2, k1] acrs.
Row 8: Same as row 2.

(Rep rows 1–8 for patt.)

shadow cable stitch

This stitch is used for the Coral and Gray Cowl Neck on page 22.

The appeal of this low-rise textured stitch is the subtle weave of the cables as they cross like shadows over the knitted fabric.

Cable 4 Back (c4b; uses 4 consecutive sts): Slip the next 2 sts onto the CN and hold them in back of the work. K2 from the LN, return the sts from the CN to the LN in reverse order, being careful not to twist the sts, then k2.

Cable 4 Front (c4f; uses 4 consecutive sts): Slip the next 2 sts onto the CN and hold them in front of the work. K2 from the LN, return sts from CN to LN in reverse order, being careful not to twist the sts, then k2.

(Multiple of 8 sts + 2)
Row 1 and all odd-numbered-rows: P acrs.
Row 2: (RS): K acrs.
Row 4: K1, *c4b, k4; rep from * to last st, k1.
Row 6: K acrs.
Row 8: K5, *c4f, k4; rep from * to last 5 sts, c4f, k1.

Rep rows 1–8 for patt.)

crocus bud stitch

This stitch is used for the Lacy Shrug with Fur Collar and Cuff on page 44.

One of the most charming stitches, the crocus bud stitch resembles the dainty flower for which it is named. Short petals rise from a short horizontal bar. Taken together, the crocus buds form a kind of garden on the knitted fabric.

Yarn over (yo): after a k st, bring the yarn to the front between the needles, then to the right and back behind the RN. The yarn is now in position for the next k st. This is one method of increasing the number of stitches in a row.

(Multiple of 2 sts + 1)
Row 1: (RS): K1; [yo, k2] acrs.
Row 2: P4; with the LN bring the third st on the RN over the first 2 sts and off; [p3; with the LN bring the third st on the RN over the first 2 sts and off] acrs.
Row 3: [K2, yo] acrs to the last st; k1.
Row 4: [P3; with the LN bring the third st on the RN over the first 2 sts and off] acrs to last st; p1.

(Rep rows 1–4 for patt.)

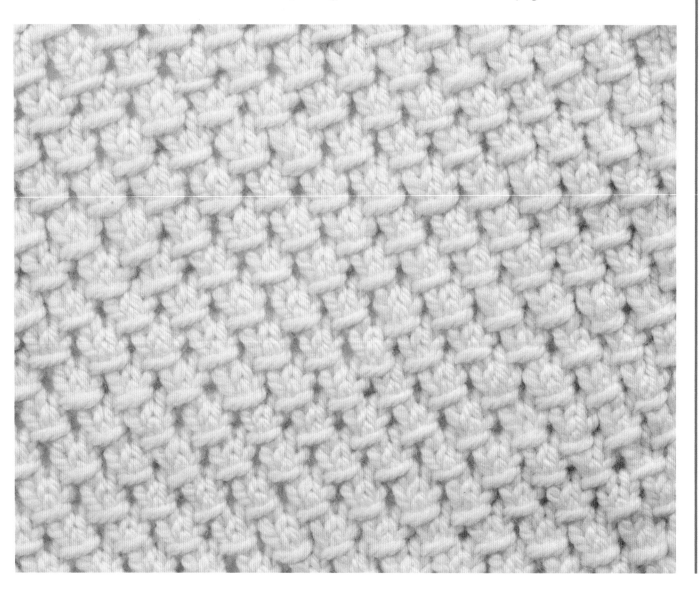

sources and resources

Berroco, Inc.
Elmdale Rd.
Uxbridge, MA 01569
www.berroco.com

Boye Needles/Wrights
South St.
W. Warren, MA 01092
(413) 436-7732
www.wrights.com

Brown Sheep Col, Inc.
100662 Country Rd. 16
Scottsbluff, NE 69361
(308) 635-2198

Cascade Yarns
1224 Andover Park East
Tukwila, WA 98188
www.cascadeyarns.com

Cherry Tree Hill Yarn
52 Church St.
Barton, VT 05822
(802) 525-3311

Coats & Clark
Consumer Services
P.O. Box 12229
Greeneville, SC 29612
(800) 648-1479
www.coatsandclark.com

Crystal Palace Yarns
160 23rd St.
Richmond, CA 94804
www.straw.com/cpy

Dale of Norway, Inc.
6W23390 Stonebridge Dr.,
Waukesha, WI 53186
(262) 544-1996

Elite Yarns
300 Jackson St.
Lowell, MA 01852
(978) 453-2837

Herrschners Inc.
2800 Hoover Rd.
Stevens Point, WI 54481
www.herrschners.com

JCA Inc.
35 Scales Lane
Townsend, MA 01469
(978) 597-3002

JKL Needles
www.jklneedles.com
Sells needles, hooks, kits, and
accessories for the knitting
enthusiast.

Knitting Fever Inc.
PO Box 502
Roosevelt, New York 11575
Tel: (516) 546 3600
www.knittingfever.com

Lion Brand Yarn Company
34 West 15th St.
New York, NY 10011
(212) 243-8995
www.lionbrand.com

M&J Trimming
1008 6th Ave.
New York, NY 10018
(800) 965-8746
www.mjtrim.com

Muench Yarns, Inc.
1323 Scott St.
Petaluma, CA 94954
(800) 733-9276
www.muenchyarns.com

Personal Threads
8025 West Dodge Rd.
Omaha, NE 68114
(800) 3306-7733
www.personalthreads.com

Purl
137 Sullivan St.
New York, NY 10012
(212) 420-8796

sources and resources

Red Heart® Yarns
Two Lakepointe Plaza
4135 So. Stream Blvd.
Charlotte, NC 28217
www.coatsandclark.com

Rowan USA/Westminister Fibers, Inc.
4 Townsend West, Unit 8
Nashua, NH 03063
(603) 886-5041
www.knitrowan.com

Solutia/Acrilan® Fibers
320 Interstate N. Pkwy.
Suite 500
Atlanta, GA 30339
www.themartyarns.com

TMA Yarns
206 W. 140th St.
Los Angeles, CA 90061

Trendsetter Yarns
16742 Stagg St.
Van Nuys, CA 91406
(818) 780-5497

Unique Knitkraft
257 West 39th St.
New York, NY 10018
212 840-6950
www.buttons.tv

Unique Kolours
23 North Bacton Hill Rd.
Malvern, PA 19355
(610) 280-7720

The Yarn Directory
www.yarndex.com
Offers an extensive yarn-selection database.

Yarn Market
www.yarnmarket.com
Sells a wide variety of yarns.

Yarns and …
26440 Southfield Rd.
Lower Level #3
Lathrup Village, MI 48076
(800) 520-9267
www.yarns-and.com

DESIGNER

Kim Hanes
kimsfiberart@netscape.net

INFORMATIONAL WEBSITES

The Knitting Guild Association (TKGA)
www.tkga.com
Offers knitting courses and information regarding knitting shows and conferences.

Onlineconversion.com
www.onlineconversion.com
Instantly converts American measurements to metric and vice versa.

Yarnstandards.com
www.yarnstandards.com
Maintains the Standard Yarn Weight System, which determines categories of yarn, gauge ranges, and recommended needle and hook sizes.

INSTRUCTIONAL WEBSITES

About.com
knitting.about.com
Offers an abundance of information about knitting, including the Knitting Stitch Library, with photos and instructions for a number of stitch patterns.

Annie's Attic
www.anniesattic.com
Features knitting and sewing instructions, with videos.

Knittinghelp.com
www.knittinghelp.com
Offers free downloadable knitting videos, with narration. Videos are also available for purchase, including the highly recommended "Circular Knitting."

index

index

acknowlegments

Although I am credited as the author, *Knit Style* was truly a cooperative effort; many talented people provided expertise and support throughout the entire developmental process. I am grateful for the privilege of naming and thanking these individuals for their indispensable contributions.

Many thanks go to Susan Haviland of Lion Brand Yarn Company, who generously provided a large sampling of yarn. Additionally, Susan was kind enough to help me meet a deadline by expertly knitting the Classic Beret, even though she surely had her own deadlines to meet.

To Kim Hanes, another angel who came to the rescue, thank you. Exceptionally creative and experienced in a variety of crafts, Kim designed and knitted two of the projects: the Ballet Sweater and the Fingerless Gloves.

Also, thank you to Karin Strom for her professional insights and for bringing the talented Eve Ng and Cheryl Krementz into the project; they are responsible for making the knitting directions accurate and decipherable.

To Damian Sandone, whose photography glows with beauty and style on each page of the book, and to Halston Bruce, Sheila Fedele, Alberto Machuca, Diane Mellina, Wanda Melendez, Gabrielle N. Sterbenz, Lee Harper, and Dana Robitz, thanks for being such an extraordinary team of pros. Thanks also to models Pat Tracey, Carina Wretman, and Kimberly Piscopo from the Wilhelmina Agency; to Mayte Arguello from the Major Agency; to Maggie Sands from the APM Agency; and especially to Molly Hinton, "star on the rise." Enormous thanks to photographers, Marta and Ben Curry, whose informative and beautiful photography enlightens "Knitting Basics" and especially to Marta who was willing to model her knitting skills and her graceful hands.

Glee Barre, Senior Designer, of Creative Homeowner did marvelous work designing the pages, as did Stephanie Phelan who made the back of the book look beautiful. Thanks, too, to Robyn Poplasky, talented photo editor; Diane P. Smith-Gayle, who drew the patterns; and Evan Lambert, who copyedited the pages of *Knit Style*.

I would be remiss if I didn't mention two family members who were instrumental in events leading up to the book. First, I would like to thank my sister-in-law Kris Jeffery for reminding me how much I enjoyed knitting and for inspiring me to revive my long-neglected knitting skills. To Linda Sims, my sister, I am extremely grateful for the recommendation she gave to her friend Senior Editor Carol Endler Sterbenz, who in turn took me on the wildest, but most exhilarating, ride of my life.

It is impossible to heap enough praise on Carol, whose creativity, experience, and multiple talents permeate each page of this book. I am grateful for the opportunity to work with such a pro, who happens to be a lovely person and to whom I owe so much gratitude.

I would be remiss if I didn't mention how much I depended on my daughter, Emily Larson, not only for her fashion and artistic advice, but also for helping with project design and construction. Huge thanks for your help, but most of all, thanks for being my number one cheerleader.

And finally, I am deeply grateful to my husband, Andy, who assumed total responsibility for running our household so I could devote time to this project. It is no exaggeration to say that without his help, I could not have authored this book. Thanks for unselfishly and enthusiastically supporting me during this singular experience, just as you always have for the past 34 years.

If you like Knit Style

take a look at other titles in our Home Arts Series

The Decorated Bag and Glamorous Beaded Jewelry

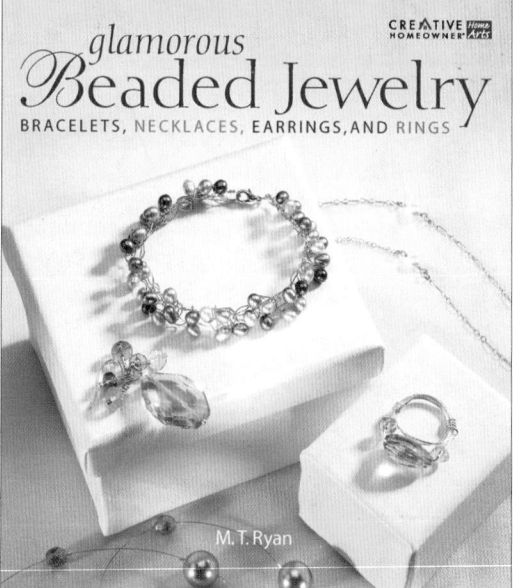

The Decorated Bag
ISBN: 1-58011-296-X
UPC: 0-78585-11296-8
CH Book # 265138
144 pages, 8½" x 9½"
$19.95 US / $24.95 CAN

**Glamorous
Beaded Jewelry**
ISBN: 1-58011-295-1
UPC: 0-78585-11295-1
CH Book # 265133
144 pages, 8½" x 9½"
$19.95 US / $24.95 CAN

The Decorated Bag is a fun and stylish collection of 50 fabulous bags that are decorated using embellishments such as sparkling rhinestones and crystals, cool pom-poms, gorgeous jewelry, faux fur, and ribbons and trims of every description.
• Over 175 original full-color images and step-by-step photographs accompanied by directions for all of the decorative techniques, explained in user-friendly language and suited to all skill levels, especially the beginner
• 25 beautiful and stylish bags PLUS another 25 design variations, including patterns for making the clutch-, pull-string-, and tote-style designs from scratch
• Author, Genevieve A. Sterbenz, is a well-known designer and television personality.

Glamorous Beaded Jewelry presents a stunning collection of 25 fun and sophisticated beaded originals—from bracelets and necklaces to rings and earrings—that you can make yourself using the infinite array of gorgeous beads available.
• Over 175 gorgeous color photographs of the stunning designs, and easy-to-follow step-by-step directions that guide even the beginner to pieces of jewelry that sparkle with style
• Features chunky bracelets, knotted-and-bejewelled chokers, chandelier earrings, lariat-style necklaces, crystal rings, and much, much more
• Special sections, including the essential "Beading Basics" and "Sources and Resources," that near-guarantee professional-looking results in jewelry-making

Look for these and other fine **Creative Homeowner** books wherever books are sold.

For more information and to order direct, go to **www.creativehomeowner.com**